VENZANO

VENZANO

a scented garden in tuscany

stephanie donaldson

NEW HOLLAND

This book is dedicated to ~
Don Leevers & Lindsay Megarrity

First published in 2001 by New Holland Publishers (UK) Ltd
London • Cape Town • Sydney • Auckland

Garfield House, 86-88 Edgware Road, London W2 2EA, United Kingdom

80 McKenzie Street, Cape Town 8001, South Africa

Level 1, Unit 4, 14 Aquatic Drive, Frenchs Forest, NSW 2086, Australia

218 Lake Road, Northcote, Auckland, New Zealand

ISBN 1 85974 590 3

EDITOR: Susan Berry
PHOTOGRAPHY: Michelle Garrett and Sue Snell
DESIGN: Debbie Mole
MAP ILLUSTRATION: Jim Robins
PRODUCTION: Caroline Hansell
EDITORIAL DIRECTION: Yvonne McFarlane

10 9 8 7 6 5 4 3 2 1

Reproduction by COLOURSCAN
Printed and bound in Singapore by Kyodo Printing Co (Pte) Ltd

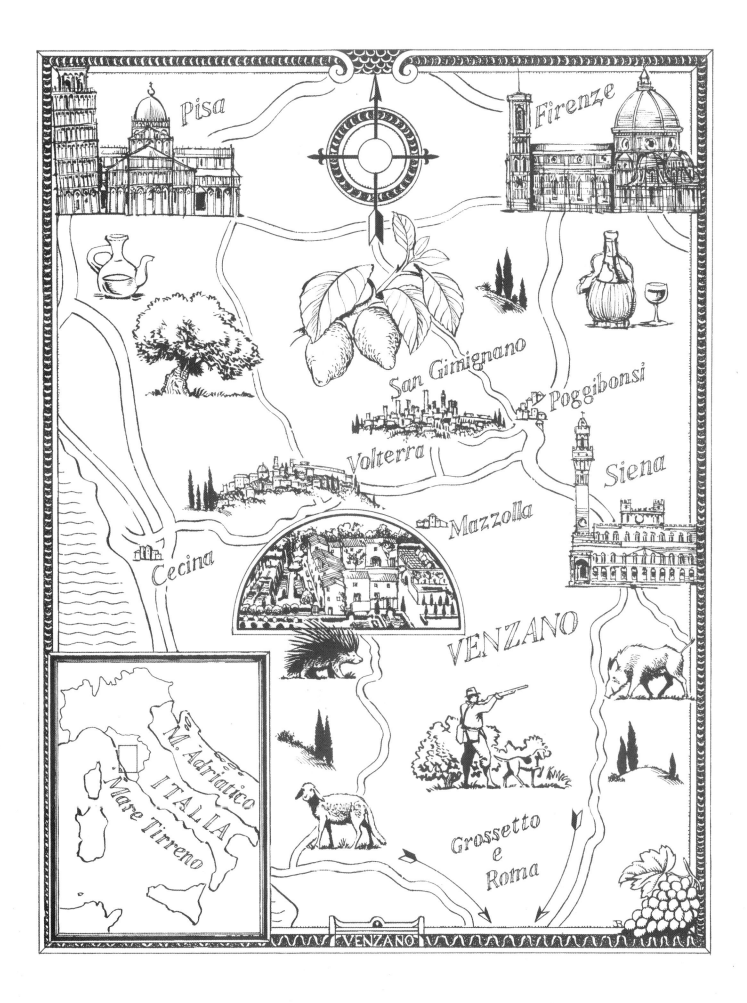

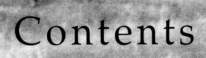

Contents

Introduction

HIDDEN AWAY AT THE END of a dusty *strada bianca* which twists and turns through the dramatic landscape of western Tuscany, there is an unexpectedly fertile fold in the hills. It holds within it a garden of the senses.

Ancient trees and vine-clad pergolas shade the visitor from the searing summer sun, and the sweet water that rises at the 2500-year-old Etruscan spring quenches the fiercest thirst. Walking around the garden, your fingers brush against the fragrant foliage of the aromatic plants that line every path and tall lily flowers lean inwards and envelop you in their scent. The sound of cicadas fills the air, while brightly coloured butterflies and diligent bees flit from flower to flower. In a moment of sensory overload, it becomes clear that this garden – Venzano – is an earthly paradise.

It is beautiful but not grand, many of the buildings are in ruins, and the life here is simple and sometimes quite hard. For centuries, it was an Augustinian monastery before being closed down on the orders of Napoleon, following which it was rented out by the church and tenanted by farmers. It fell into increasing disrepair until rescued in 1986 by Don Leevers and his partner, Lindsay Megarrity.

Venzano is a place that has drawn me back again and again – and I am not alone in this enchantment. Many of those who stay in the apartments are annual visitors for whom one or two weeks at Venzano are the perfect escape from the pressures of their everyday lives. But why Venzano? There are certainly far grander places to stay, with all the attendant delights of satellite television, maid service, swimming pools and tennis courts, but at Venzano you don't feel like a temporary tenant in a holiday villa. Instead, you feel involved in what is happening – with the place, the people and the plants. On return visits you admire a newly erected wall, and perhaps comment on how quickly the latest planting has established itself. You even find yourself feeling irritated when a carload of people spends an entire afternoon examining every inch of the garden and then leave without buying a single plant.

I have visited Venzano in spring, summer and autumn. Each season has its own special magic, but, to my mind, Venzano is at its most beautiful in the late spring or early summer when roses cascade over pergolas and walls, the dianthus are in full bloom, the thyme plants are smothered with flowers and wild flowers carpet the verges. This book is mainly about the garden during this lovely season, but it also records the changes that take place during summer and autumn. In winter, Venzano becomes a private domain and I have not intruded on this privacy.

To those who may be tempted to follow in my footsteps, a word of warning: Venzano's beauty is a subtle thing, not readily appreciated by those who drop in for the odd hour or two when they are "doing Tuscany". It is a working nursery as well as a beautiful garden, so there are untidy corners, functional working areas and much that has yet to be developed. The expectation is that those who call in are genuine plant lovers, and will, whenever possible, actually buy some plants or, at the very least, express their gratitude for what they have seen.

This book is a personal appreciation of both the people and the place, which have become special to me. Although its situation and history may be unique, there are other gardens out there equally deserving of close acquaintance.

May you find the garden which touches your heart in the way that Venzano has touched mine.

right: *Although much of his time is now spent designing gardens and managing projects, Don is, above all, a hands-on gardener who loves nothing better than to spend time working amongst his plants. These days, he finds that opportunities for this type of work happens more often in his clients' gardens than at Venzano.*

opposite (above): *Lindsay at work in his studio. The meticulous detail requires many hours of work on a single flower – a back-breaking task which has led to Lindsay adopting a standing position when he paints.*

opposite (below): *The tools of Lindsay's trade stand ready for when he can steal away to his studio and paint.*

The Central Characters - Don & Lindsay

A SKILFUL AND AMUSING conversationalist, as well as a knowledgeable gardener, Don Leevers willingly shares his knowledge of plants with those who express interest. Interspersed amongst the useful information will be fascinating and often amusing anecdotes about Venzano, the neighbours and the vagaries of Italian life. To his regret, he now spends a considerable amount of time away from Venzano working for clients and has not been able to do any real work on the gardens for the last year and a half. Since this garden consultancy is classed as a second income it is so heavily taxed that effectively every second day worked is for the benefit of the government!

Although both partners are Australian, Don is the one who retains continuing links with the home country, returning each year for a month after Christmas. All Don's family are talented gardeners, the five children following on from their mother and grandfather. On visits to Venzano, his mother is put to work at the potting bench where she proves a willing and valuable helper. She is thrilled and amazed by his Italian venture. Although not a gardener, his father has passed on to Don a great love of trees – he is enormously grateful to him for opening his eyes to their extraordinary beauty and variety.

Don's sister Kim, inspired by his example, has established a nursery in Hunter Valley, Australia which, like Venzano, specializes in aromatic and scented plants. Each year, Don takes plants out to Kim, a procedure which sends Australian customs officers into a flat spin. One year they were so bemused that they suggested he take the plants away with him for the night and bring them back the next day. He pointed out that this rather defeated the point as the plants are supposed to be treated with bromide and kept in quarantine for six months.

Lindsay Megarrity is the quieter of the two. In an arrangement not entirely to his liking, he does the day to day running of the gardens, deals with the management of the apartments and sells plants to customers. Attentive to both guests and visitors, he offers advice to those who need help choosing plants but as soon as his duty is done, he returns to his first love, painting. Most days, he manages to spend a few hours in his studio. Throughout his life at Venzano, Lindsay has found time to produce his meticulously detailed and exquisitely painted botanical illustrations which continue to win awards and are regularly exhibited at galleries around the world.

He is extraordinarily modest about his talents and it will often take repeated requests to persuade him to show his work. His studio is strictly off-limits to any visitors, so

at a pre-arranged time he will shyly emerge with a selection of his most recent paintings. Looking at Lindsay's work engenders a sense of awe at the hours and hours of labour each painting represents, at the commitment, accuracy and powers of observation involved. Given his daily workload at Venzano it is astonishing that he ever finds time to complete such detailed botanical illustrations.

Before finding Venzano, Don and Lindsay had already lived in Europe for many years. Initially based in England, Lindsay worked as a set designer in film and theatre and Don travelled to far-flung places for his work as a geologist. At that time, gardening was no more than a pleasant pastime between jobs, much enjoyed by both of them, in their Herefordshire country garden. However, a seed of an idea began to germinate and they planned a different future for themselves. Don was tiring of the endless travelling and Lindsay's skills as a botanical artist were gaining strength, confirmed by the award of his first Gold Medal by the Royal Horticultural Society in 1987.

THE LURE

OF TUSCANY

Looking southwards, it is apparent that the landscape around Venzano is on a larger, less populated scale than eastern Tuscany where every hill is clothed with olive groves or scrub woodland and topped by a villa. Here, the treeless hills roll away to the horizon with only the occasional building to be seen, and later exploration will reveal that many of these are uninhabited ruins. Such is the extent of the panorama that it is difficult to judge the distances involved.

How it all Began

NESTLING AMONGST TREES on the brow of a hill, Venzano overlooks a part of Tuscany where agriculture still predominates. The huge rolling fields to the south of the gardens grow grain, while smaller ones to the east are planted with olives. Steep, rocky pastures are grazed by sheep, while valleys conceal surprisingly large areas of woodland. Because of the lack of buildings it can be hard to judge distances and it is only when you set out on what appears to be a short walk that you discover that the apparently nearby hillside is in fact separated from Venzano by a river and extensive, impenetrable woodland.

Two years before buying Venzano, Don and Lindsay spent a holiday touring through Tuscany and Umbria. They loved the landscape and as they travelled around they visited estate agents and arranged for details of suitable properties to be sent to them in England. Over the months there were some promising contenders among the sheaves of details that arrived – one particular set had a tiny picture of a place which interested them very much. In passing, they read the reverse side which had the details of Venzano - but it looked as if it was still occupied by nuns or monks and appeared far too grand and expensive for their needs.

Full of optimism, engendered in part by the estate agent's hyperbole, they arranged another trip to Italy. Touring round Umbria they viewed the various properties they had selected and found them not only unsuitable but deeply impractical. Not a single property had a reliable water supply. Even if they had found somewhere quite wonderful they knew that without water it would be impossible, and Don's experience as a geologist led them to question any suggestions that water could easily be found by drilling a bore-hole.

As time went by, they began to lose heart. The endless viewing of tumbledown, waterless properties was very dispiriting. Realizing that water had to be a priority, they asked one agent, Michael Goodall (who has since become a great friend) if he knew of any properties with water. He had just one he could show them. So it was that one misty November afternoon they first came to Venzano. A photograph taken that afternoon shows Lindsay and Michael staring at the house from the courtyard, which was full of rampant vegetation including

several large trees. Overly large, derelict and too expensive, it was hardly their ideal property but something about the place aroused their curiosity and enthusiasm. Returning to their hotel that evening they were both rather quiet, considering the implications of what they had seen. Lindsay broke the silence by announcing, "I think we should buy it". Relieved to find that his feelings about Venzano were shared, Don responded, "So do I, but where are we going to find the money?"

Looking back, Don now feels that the way they found and decided to buy the place was all rather extraordinary. Seeing it on a misty day, they had no idea of the extent of the buildings or their setting. The second time they came to Venzano they were appalled by what they had done. The grey winter's day revealed it to be sitting on the brow of a hill with the whole of western Tuscany spread out before it, whereas Don's recollection was of a secret, hidden-away place. This was not an instant love affair, more a moment of madness!

On their return to England, they began to do the sums – it was going to take everything they had, and more, to raise the purchase price. They put their Herefordshire house on the market and engaged in some painfully complex financial manoeuvring to ensure that they could scrape together the money they needed. The actual purchase of Venzano was highly complicated and at times extremely nerve-wracking. Like many of their dealings with Italian bureaucracy, the process was a mystery. Once the purchase was completed, however, they were more than happy to forget the tribulations but they remain enduringly grateful to Michael for guiding them through the labyrinthine legal processes.

When the day finally arrived for the move to Italy, they packed up their house in Herefordshire, put most of their possessions into storage and loaded the basic essentials in their Renault 4. After a long drive down through Holland, Germany and northern Italy they finally arrived at Venzano as darkness fell on the evening of the 29th April, 1988. They had arranged with the previous owners that the keys would be hidden in a niche in the wall, tucked behind a terracotta tile. To their great relief they found them in the pre-arranged spot. Unlocking the door, they walked into their new home – one without running water, electricity or a telephone. That first summer they camped rather than lived at Venzano. A black plastic camping bag hung from a tree as an alfresco shower. If they waited until four in the afternoon the water reached the perfect temperature – neither too hot nor too cold. These small comforts assumed enormous importance in such primitive conditions. The bedroom was any corner of a dry room swept clean of dust and dead insects. If the roof leaked, they moved the sleeping bags to another corner, or another room. Candles lit the rooms and corridors, giving the whole place an immensely romantic air.

This type of simple life was idyllic in the summer, but became unbearable once winter arrived. One of the first investments was a petrol-driven pump to carry water from the spring to a 100-litre (25-gallon) tank in the house. The other was to purchase hurricane lamps to allow them to read when the candles proved too feeble for anything more than casting an attractive glow. It was a great relief when, within that first year, they managed to get power to Venzano. Gradually, life became marginally more civilized, but the turning point came when they could finally bring their furniture and belongings over from England. The removals men who brought all their worldly possessions on board a large truck seemed surprisingly unphased by the remoteness of the location, the bumpy drive down the three-kilometre track and the semi-ruin into which they carried the furniture. For Don and Lindsay, though, this was a highly significant moment – Venzano was now their home.

The first 18 months were also harrowing for other reasons. They could do no work of any sort on the buildings until the Commune (the local authority) gave them permission to proceed, and permission depended upon the Commune categorizing the works they were undertaking as an agricultural project. Unfortunately, the Commune seemed unable to comprehend that the nursery was just that. Without the necessary categorization of the nursery, they would not be allowed to convert some of the buildings into apartments under the "Agriturismo" arrangements which govern rural buildings in Tuscany. That 18-month wait nearly bankrupted them, as the longer the delay, the longer they would have to survive without a potential income.

In the meantime, to keep their sanity, they built stone walls in the garden. If the apartments they planned for renting out had been started, those walls would never have been built. Primitive in comparison with those they have built since, they have helped to define boundaries and provide the structure of the garden.

Around Venzano

THE FIELDS, VALLEYS AND WOODLAND that surround Venzano make up the intimate landscape that Don and Lindsay have come to know so well since they arrived in Tuscany. It's where, in rare moments of leisure, they walk down the lane for a swim in the nearby river, the Cecina, collect seeds or cuttings from native plants or resignedly watch the hunters doing their best to decimate the wildlife which abounds in the area. Although not all aspects of rural Tuscan life charm or attract them, they know that as newcomers they must respect the local ways if they are to be accepted by their neighbours.

The seasonal differences here are quite extraordinary. Immediately after harvest, the surrounding fields, and those for as far as the eye can see, are ploughed, transforming the whole area into an apparently barren moonscape in which Venzano floats like a solitary green island, kept green by its natural spring. Between the fields, deep in the folds of the valleys, ribbons of dark green woodland are the only other indication that this is a living landscape. By contrast, in the spring, Venzano is surrounded by fields of startling emerald green, the result, sadly, of profligate use of artificial fertilizers rather than natural fertility as the soil itself is extremely poor. Fortunately, Venzano's own soil is a rich sandy loam, thanks to hundreds of years of good husbandry by Augustinian monks who once worked it.

On an old pre-war field plan, which Don and Lindsay managed to track down, the names of the fields reveal their usage - *olivetto, frutteto* and *canneto* (brushwood). The plan shows that right up to the Second World War all the southern slopes surrounding Venzano were olive-clad while the others were covered in woodland. Post-war changes wrought a dramatic effect on a landscape which until then had remained largely unchanged; modern agricultural methods were introduced and the move away from mixed farming over

the intervening years gathered pace. It seems likely that these changes will continue for the foreseeable future.

Until shortly before Don and Lindsay acquired Venzano, so they were told, there was a beautiful old orchard beyond the Gravel Garden filled with ancient cherries, figs and olives. The owner of the orchard lived at some distance from Venzano and, when he found he could no longer pick the fruit himself, rather than leaving it for the enjoyment of others, he grubbed out the trees. Looking at the small, irregularly shaped, and seldom-cultivated field that now remains, it seems a tragic and unnecessary waste.

Immediately behind Venzano a steep valley falls away from the stone walls of the erstwhile monastery's northern boundary. Filled with ancient trees and creepers, with the mist rising up off it after heavy rain, the valley resembles a Brazilian rain-forest. The centre of this valley used to be occupied by an enormous and ancient oak tree. One day when Don and Lindsay were working at the other end of the garden they were stopped in their tracks by an extraordinary and unidentifiable noise. Searching round for the source, they could not, at first, make sense of the dramatic alteration to the northern skyline. Then it suddenly dawned on them what had occurred. For no apparent reason, although seemingly healthy, the oak tree had abruptly loosened its grip on the earth and crashed to the valley floor. Don was heartbroken by its loss and is reminded of it whenever he looks across the valley, which has been irrevocably altered by its departure.

below: *For anyone more used to the densely populated hills of Chianti, the relative emptiness of western Tuscany is a revelation. Off the main roads on the extensive* strade bianche *which criss-cross this area, it is possible to drive for hours without seeing another human being.*

Natural disasters, small or large, are not unusual, and this is an unforgiving landscape. In 1985 much of Tuscany, Venzano included, was devastated by terrible frosts. The mercury plunged to -26°C (-7°F) followed by ten days of freezing rain – weather so extreme for this part of the world that no records of a similar event exist. At the time, it was believed that the majority of the olive trees had been killed by the frosts, so farmers were compensated for their loss and given grants to grub the old trees out and replant them with modern varieties that could be picked by machine. As a result, the olive trees are no longer pruned into the classical cup-shape and it is doubtful whether the new trees will ever have the beautiful gnarled outline so characteristic of the old ones. Fortunately, however, many ancient olives did survive the frost and have sprouted from their bases (500 years ago the trees were selected rather than grafted so they have regrown true to form.

All is not lost, therefore, and some of these trees will once again have the opportunity to enrich the landscape in their timeless fashion. Although the old varieties probably produce only half the crop of modern cultivars, they are an invaluable gene-bank and it is vital they do not disappear. If a similar frost were to devastate the modern, grafted olive groves, the regrowth would all be from the wild olive rootstock and would therefore have no commercial use.

above: *An old wooden barrel, long pre-dating Don and Lindsay's arrival disintegrates picturesquely in the olive grove.*

opposite: *In early autumn the ripening olives give promise of a good harvest to come for Venzano.*

Venzano's own olive grove on the lower slopes is half-owned by Don and Lindsay and half-rented from a neighbour. They grow five different types of olive – *Leccino, Frantoio, Corrogilio, Maurino,* and *Moraiolo* – all of which ripen at different times and each with its own special characteristics. It is quite usual to grow a mixture of olives, which are then harvested simultaneously. The mixture of fully-ripe and semi-ripe olives gives the oil a much fruitier and livelier flavour, which is typical of Tuscan olive oils.

Beneath the olive trees, the grove is carpeted with a wonderful diversity of wild flowers from early spring through to autumn. French honeysuckle (*Hedysarum coronarium),* wild larkspur and bulbs like orchids, alliums and star of Bethlehem *(Ornithogalum)* all emerge from among the grasses at their appointed time of year. Although Don and Lindsay have no desire to tame this area, they have eliminated the blackberries and are working on the nettles with the aim of creating a managed wild environment.

The countryside around Venzano is wonderfully endowed with wild flowers – six types of orchid are common, including a tiny bee orchid and a tall-growing lady orchid with purple-pink flowers (see page 22). In the spring, the woods are carpeted with sky blue hepatica, anemones, wood sorrel and primroses. The rich diversity of the flora has survived thanks to this being something of an agricultural backwater which has had little

exposure to herbicides. They had not been used at all until about twelve years ago and, when the subsidy was removed six years later, the farmers proved unwilling to pay the full cost themselves, so the natural flora has survived remarkably intact.

The wild fauna is not so lucky. This is an area where hunting is an integral part of life, Tuscan recipe books are full of recipes for wild boar, pheasant and venison, and game dishes predominate at local restaurants. During the hunting season, four-wheel drive vehicles filled with excited men in camouflage gear accompanied by equally excited dogs bump down the lane. Once the occupants reach their appointed destination, they tumble out and disappear into the woods or stalk the field margins in search of game. Hunters are not supposed to shoot towards or within 300 m (400 yds) of a dwelling, but there has been at least one occasion when guests, enjoying the morning air at Venzano, have been alarmed to see hunters emerging from thickets below the olive groves, lift their guns and shoot towards them as some small songbird takes to the air. Fortunately, both birds and guests have escaped so far unscathed, but as Italian hunters are notorious for killing one another, caution, loud conversation and conspicuous clothing are always advisable during the hunting season.

A narrow lane bisects Venzano. Calling this rough track a 'lane' affords it a status it scarcely deserves.

above (left): *Don and Lindsay found this wild sweet pea with its striking sky blue and purple flowers and intense fragrance growing in the valley below the house. It now self-seeds happily around the gardens.*

above (centre): *Stately lady orchids grow along the margins of the lane and also in the surrounding mead.*

above (right): *A diminutive bee orchid nestles on the verges, invisible to all but the sharpest eyes.*

opposite: The gloriously rampant Cooper's Burmese rose threatens to engulf parts of the house. Although not frost-hardy, it clearly has no trouble surviving and thriving at Venzano.

Immediately outside the buildings large lumps of bedrock protrude from the dusty ruts and in wet weather it becomes more a rocky stream than a lane. Still, this does mean that the (blessedly occasional) passing vehicles are forced to a virtual halt as they negotiate their way around the rocks. If it is late spring or early summer, the drivers may well be tempted to stop completely, the better to admire the spectacle of Venzano's Cooper's Burmese rose in full bloom. It is a magnificent climber with very large single white flowers and extremely glossy evergreen foliage, regrettably only once-flowering, although it does remain in bloom for several weeks. The Italians have proved to be very enthusiastic about climbing roses and Cooper's Burmese has proved irresistible – although customers from further north are advised against it as it is too tender for colder climates. The rose has only been there for eight years and has already been severely cut back as it had completely covered the roof above the studio apartments, lifting the tiles in the process. Its roots have found their way into an old septic tank which may partly account for the prodigious growth.

Beyond the rose, the lane drops gently downhill as it passes the Gravel Garden which is hidden behind the luxuriant growth and stately trunks of the robinias. They are attractive trees especially in the late spring when they are in full, fragrant bloom,

right: *Bordering the lane, ancient pomegranate trees grow out of the terrace walls, survivors from the monastic gardens. The trees bear waxy flowers in spring that set into fruit which eventually reach the size of oranges.*

opposite (above): *The drooping petals of a rain-washed evening primrose (Oenothera odorata) which blushes a soft apricot pink as it matures.*

opposite (below): *Freshly opened flowers on the same evening primrose plant are a creamy yellow and exude a delicious lemon scent into the evening air.*

although they are far from ideal trees for a garden because of their habit of sending up great bunches of suckers from the slightest scrape to their roots. The flowers are traditionally used to make a Tuscan delicacy – *fritelle di fiori di acacia* – dipped in a light batter and deep-fried, before being served sprinkled with sugar. Later in the year, at the end of autumn, low-growing clumps of flowers will glow an unseasonal bright yellow below the robinias. These are *Sternbergia lutea*, with deep yellow crocus-like flowers clustered among deep green leaves. Sternbergia is a member of the daffodil family and a native plant of this area.

Nestled into the base of the robinias are the only trees to survive from monastic times. Four extremely ancient pomegranates with their gnarled and misshapen branches emerge from the old stone wall and are thought to be 300 years old. In spite of their great age and their curious shape, they remain productive, bearing a good crop of fruit "as large as babies heads", so Don says. (According to Lindsay this is a favourite expression of Don's and the claim is best ignored as he is prone to exaggeration.)

Once past the buildings, the lane meanders on, overhung by jasmine which must have escaped from the monastery centuries ago. At about this point the lane abandons all pretence of being a thoroughfare and degenerates into a farm track leading down to a wooded valley and the river.

In the spring the woods are loud with birdsong and the rustle of foraging animals while the margins of the track are resplendent with a wonderful array of wildflowers, tassel hyacinth (*Muscari comosum*) with their weirdly wonderful top-knots, crown anemone (*Anemone coronaria*), pheasant's eye (*Adonis annua*), birthwort (*Aristolochia rotunda*), and sainfoin (*Onobrychis viciifolia*) and field marigold (*Calendula arvensis*), as well as swathes of creeping thyme and clusters of orchids.

If you venture into the woodlands in the autumn after the hunters have departed, clusters of wild cyclamen can be seen glowing in the gloom while in the open, alongside the track, long-stemmed daisies nod their delicate heads and furl their petals as the light fades to reveal their deep pink undersides. The lane finally peters out at the bottom of the valley where it meets up with several similar tracks which converge on the river while a small pathway continues a little further to a ruined house in the shade of an ancient walnut tree.

Mazzolla

above (left): *A pot of arum lilies (Zantedeschia aethiopica) stands next to the front door of a village house.*

above (centre): *The old cart-track to the village still has some surviving cypresses marking its route.*

above (right): *A chair stands ready for an occupant in the village square. Once the heat has abated the residents will emerge for their evening gossip.*

THERE IS A T-JUNCTION at the end of the *strada bianca* which leads away from Venzano towards the main road. Turn left onto the tarmac and you will soon be on the busy road that leads to Volterra or Colle di Val d'Elsa, turn right and the only destination is Mazzolla. Perched on a rocky outcrop, Mazzolla is more hamlet than village; clustered around the square there is a church, a few houses and a restaurant but there is no room for anything more atop the hill. Visitors are well-advised to park in the car park half-way up the hill or risk either having to reverse round some very tricky bends or adopt other equally challenging manoeuvres if the square is full. As you walk up the hill there is the accompanying distant melody of sheep bells, and in day-light hours the opportunity to stop and admire the view; at night, unless there is a moon, all will be darkness except for the occasional twinkling light in the distance.

A short walk is good preparation for a meal at the restaurant which will be simple, inexpensive, and very good. This is real country food with portions substantial enough to defeat even hearty appetites. The emphasis is on meat, especially game: wild boar, venison, rabbit and hare are all on the menu and the heads of some of their departed relatives stare down from the walls – not a place for the sensitive vegetarian.

Mazzolla is a million miles away from the bustle of nearby towns: there are no shops selling tourist tat or local produce, nor is the architecture either notable or particularly attractive. In many ways, its mediocrity, combined with the lack of parking, has protected it and ensured that it remains a small, unspoiled Tuscan hamlet. Unlike its counterparts further east, western Tuscany abounds with such blessedly ordinary, little-visited villages where life remains much as it has done over many centuries.

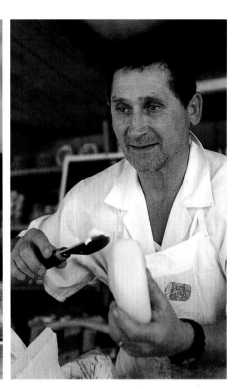

Volterra and Beyond

TEN MINUTES' DRIVE from Venzano, Volterra is a brooding presence which looms over the surrounding landscape. Perched on top of a long-extinct volcano, it appears from the outside a forbidding city, its medieval fortifications seemingly impenetrable. Inside the city walls the tall buildings keep the streets in shade – a boon in summer, but very cold at times during the winter. The streets are lined with numerous shops selling the local alabaster, much of it hardly worth a second glance, but, even in the most unpromising premises, you can often find a small, perfect, translucent bowl or an exquisitely simple vase.

In the museum, among the many Etruscan artefacts, there is an extraordinarily beautiful tall, thin, bronze figure which could almost have been sculpted by Giacometti. It is called "Ombra della Sera" which translates as "Evening Shadow" and is believed to be a 3rd-century BC Etruscan votive figure. Its recent history is far more banal – a farmer ploughed it up in his field and used it as a handy poker. Fortunately for art-lovers, someone recognized it as a priceless piece of Etruscan art. Now replicas of "Ombra della Sera" can be found in every gift shop in the area.

The Saturday market at Volterra is, quite literally, a movable feast. From late spring until early autumn it takes place outside the city walls in what remains of the Roman amphitheatre, while for the rest of the year it moves into two of the central squares. Whichever location, the market is a visual delight as well as a source of much wonderful food. Kaleidoscopic displays of fruit and vegetables, familiar and unfamiliar, fill the stalls. In spite of European laws that seem intent on standardizing the appearance of everything that is sold, there is a wonderful variability in the produce sold here. An old van, parked in the corner, is piled high with lumpy

above (left): *Local apricots may not have the standard uniformity so beloved of supermarkets, but their flavour is ambrosial.*

above (centre): *Cheese stalls are piled high with a magnificent selection of the local parmesans and pecorinos.*

above (right): *No cheese is bought untasted – both stallholders and customers enjoy the ritual of the purchase.*

right: Cherry trees abound in the country-side around Venzano and during their season the market stalls are piled high with the juicy black fruit. A bowl of these luscious ripe fruit needs no accompaniment other than perhaps a glass of chilled prosecco.

above: Most vegetables at Volterra's market are grown locally by small-scale growers who pride themselves on the quality of their produce. Sweet red onions are perfect in the traditional Tuscan salad of cannellini beans and tuna dressed with olive oil.

organic melons and mellow, golden grapes while a small stall, wedged between the larger operators, is presided over by an elderly woman who proudly displays a few bunches of home-grown flowers, eggs, a couple of plucked chickens, garlic and some young plants. Women like her have been displaying similar modest wares in this market for centuries – long before the professional stallholders came into being. In earlier times, the van driver would probably have been selling his melons and grapes from his cart.

Custom-made vans, which transform themselves into specialist food counters, are parked alongside the fruit and vegetable stalls. Two are piled high with an array of cheeses that would make the serious cheese-fancier faint with desire. Huge parmesans and granas of various vintages and provenances take centre stage and a short wedge-shaped tool is used to break off lumps which are accepted or rejected by the cognoscenti in a way that is totally unfathomable to the outsider.

Nearby, the central display on a cooked-meat stall consists of an enormous stuffed and rolled joint of pork called *porchetta*. It is cooked to a golden perfection and looks quite delicious, but, be warned, the stuffing consists entirely of salt with a few added herbs and is definitely an acquired taste. A separate area is devoted to those universal marketplace wares – cheap shoes and handbags, poorly made clothing, bed linen, tablecloths and vast displays of kitchen utensils. Careful examination of the goods can reveal the occasional genuine bargain, but the delectable food stalls of Volterra market are where the real treasure lies. In winter, the exhibition of wild mushrooms (for the purpose of identification) is worth a visit.

Hereabouts, going to the market is women's work. The men have much more important things to do. They must stand around outside the offices of the local communist party (Volterra is fiercely communist) or sit in bars and cafés and put the world to rights. While the women shop, the men gesticulate and argue until their wives arrive, fully laden, and take their husbands home ready for another week of class struggle!

Discovering Venzano

ONLY THE DETERMINED and the well-directed will find Venzano. Guests and visitors alike exchange tales of lost hours as they searched in vain for the road to Venzano. Negotiating the tortuous twists of the road between Colle di Val d'Elsa and Volterra, with its spectacular views of western Tuscany, it is all too easy to miss the small road on the left which leads to the nearby hamlet of Mazzolla.

The first few hundred metres of tarmac give no hint of what is to come. Just as you finish congratulating yourself on having successfully found the turning, the road deteriorates into a crumbling relic of its former self, albeit still lined with the characteristic sentinel cypresses. The driver cannot afford the luxury of admiring the landscape or stealing glances at the abundant flora and fauna of the verges; large areas of the road threaten to break away down vertiginous drops on one side or the other. For the uninitiated, this is a drive which supplies some heart-stopping moments, especially when you have to wrench the car away from the centre of the thoroughfare to make way for a speeding vehicle hurtling towards you as if this apology for a road was actually the Florence-Siena autostrada.

Two kilometres along the road a sign, so modest as to be well-nigh invisible, directs you to Venzano down a rough, rutted track. At times, this appears to lead nowhere other than a dilapidated farmyard or barn; but, on each occasion, the track curves away at the last moment and leads deeper into this hidden corner of Tuscany. Here, the landscape is less extreme, the sloping meadows bordering the track tenanted by flocks of sheep that are guarded day and night by Maremanno sheep dogs. Large and white, they blend inconspicuously with the sheep until a perceived threat arrives on the scene, whereupon they peel off from the flock, barking and snarling like veritable wolves in sheep's clothing. They are ever vigilant, for no matter what hour you may pass, they will be there to see you on your way.

Necessarily slow progress along the track gives you plenty of time to observe the natural flora. In spring the verges are carpeted with extraordinary array of flowers including scarlet pheasant's eye, deep bue tassel hyacinths, scarlet anemones, and orchids. All are blended in a colourful tapestry, punctuated by the spiky grey leaves of the wild artichoke. Wild artichoke? It is is a moment of revelation when you realize that the carefully cosseted garden artichoke has a wild relative growing happily on the rocky roadside verges of Tuscany.

Three kilometres further down the track, when you have all but given up hope of ever finding Venzano, the road tucks itself between high banks bordered by olive groves. Wild thyme, giant fennel, cistus, marjoram and honeysuckle grow in aromatic profusion among the rampant brambles that line the track and threaten to envelop any passing car. Just when it seems as if Sleeping Beauty's castle cannot be far away, the track widens and your persistence is rewarded: you reach journey's end – Venzano.

previous page (left):
*Spiky wild artichokes
are as common as other
members of the thistle
family in some pastures.*
previous page (right):
*A discreet sign tacked
onto a tree trunk at the
start of the rough track
is the only indication
that the visitor is on the
right road.*
this page: *The local
Sardinian shepherd
and his Maremanno
sheepdog take the sheep
back to their pastures
after milking.*

Venzano's History

SINCE THEIR ARRIVAL, Don and Lindsay have worked hard to uncover as much as possible about the history of Venzano, which, although unrecorded, goes back to well before the 10th century. The area is thought to have been inhabited by the Etruscans, a little known people who date back to pre-Roman times and whom the Romans finally conquered. Not much is known about their history, and their obliteration, interestingly, was brought about by cultural rather than physical genocide. Their language was forbidden and so total was this ban that within 50 years only a few scholars retained any knowledge of it. No books survive in the language so it remains something of a mystery. There is little real evidence of the nature of Etruscan culture other than fragments and thus far nothing specifically Etruscan has been found at Venzano.

With the arrival of the Romans things became a little more certain. There must have been a Roman inhabitation on the site (possibly a temple) because of the spring and the fact that white travertine blocks from a Roman quarry near San Giminignano have been used in the building of the house. The name itself – Venzano – has clear Roman links. After the Roman Civil War in the 3rd century AD, victorious centurions were given grants of arable land in the area and place names ending with "-ano" indicate a Roman habitation. The centurion in Venzano's case is believed to have been called Arvensius.

Whatever its antecedents, it is one of the oldest isolated forms of rural building still surviving in the area, and there is evidence that it was one of the monasteries on the pilgrimage route to Rome. The site was given to the church in 1008 by Marchese Guiscardo and remained the property of the Augustinian Order until 1971, although the monastic order was closed down by Napoleon on 31 March, 1811, and the property subsequently

above (left):
Previously reclaimed floor tiles are stacked ready for use when the need arises.

above (right):
In the course of earlier restoration they uncovered old manuscripts, a newspaper dated 1871 and a violin bow.

opposite (left):
The bell-tower above the chapel betrays Venzano's ecclesiastical past.

opposite (right):
The fresco of St. Andrew in Venzano's chapel.

let out to tenant farmers by the church. Prior to that, Venzano was a farming community of monks, growing fruit and olives, and grapes which were turned into wine for the church at Volterra. There was a vineyard in front of the house, a vegetable garden below the spring and, down the road, an olive grove on the southern slope, below which, according to the map, was *il genestroja*, the field where the broom for lighting the bread oven was cultivated.

The earliest part of the building – the south side nearest the lane – was originally a 13th-century Romanesque chapel, many times rebuilt. It ceased to be a chapel sometime during the 14th and 15th centuries, when the rest of the building was added. The U-shape of the buildings is very unusual for the area, but monastries never seem to have been built entirely symmetrically – bits were added on as the need arose. The tower in the north-west corner was originally called a villa – an unusual feature in ecclesiastic settlements. Later it became the *cantina* (wine-making area) with an extraordinary curved doorway specially adapted to accommodate barrels.

The current chapel, the Oratorio de San Macario, with its fresco of St Andrew (San Macario was one of his followers), probably dates from the late 17th century. When Don and Lindsay arrived at Venzano, it was completely ruined with a hole in the roof and most of the plaster gone, but with just enough surviving to divine the original patterns. Now renovated, the painted Sienese block-work is restored to its former splendour, as is the blue sky scattered with gold stars.

Some years ago, John Pope Hennessy, the famous art historian and already a very old man, came to visit Venzano accompanied by an equally eminent and equally ancient companion. The companion demanded that Pope Hennessy examine the mural. After a considerable struggle to make it up the steps to the chapel, this he did. After some deliberation, however, they both decided that the fresco, although in good condition, was not of very good quality, leaving Don with the distinct impression that they very much regretted all the effort and energy expended on the visit!

In earlier times a visit to the chapel would have been much more rewarding. A fine painting of the 14th-century Madonna of Venzano by Benedetto of Siena used to hang there but it was removed when the chapel was deconsecrated. A holy relic still remains, set into the altar, and in front of it is the wooden platform on which the priest celebrated mass. If it is lifted, the date 1778 can be seen painted on the underside.

Between the dissolution of the monastery in 1811 and its sale in September 1971 to a family of Sicilian farmers, Venzano endured a chequered history. At one time, there were four tenants in the property and later the house was abandoned for nearly 30 years – so it is extraordinary that the chapel has survived to the extent it has.

Creating Venzano

O NCE DON AND LINDSAY arrived at Venzano, the enormity of what they had done became apparent as they grasped the sheer scale of the work in store. Even now, over a decade later, there are rooms which have yet to be tackled and the contrast between the adjoining, perfectly appointed apartments and their own simple, rustic home is quite startling. There are plans for central heating and a comfortably furnished sitting room, but in the meantime they make do with the open fire in the kitchen and a pair of battered old armchairs shared with the cats. Renovating a property like Venzano is a combination of hard work and occasional happy accidents – their kitchen being an excellent example. The fireplace was re-instated after a piece of plaster fell off what turned out to be a false wall, revealing the original fireplace behind it.

As they worked clearing the gardens around the buildings, Don and Lindsay had time to get to know their new home and to understand the materials from which it had been constructed. Most of the stones used in building Venzano had been quarried out of the courtyard and from a bank which probably stood where the buildings at the rear of the courtyard now stand. When the courtyard was cleared of trees, briars, brambles and weeds, they were delighted to uncover a paved surface 60 cm (2 ft) below the surface of the soil. This probably dates from 1800 when the barn which adjoins the main house was built – they know the date because the inscription of the Abbott was hand-painted on the top of a column but unfortunately this was lost during restoration. According to local rumour there is a well in the courtyard, but Don is extremely dubious about this as much of the surface of the courtyard is made up of bedrock.

The extensive cellar under the main house is reached through the back of the building and is one of the earliest parts

right: When they first arrived at Venzano, the Courtyard was all but obscured after years of neglect. Self-sown trees, brambles and other weeds grew rampantly and the paved surface was yet to be revealed.

of the monastery. There is a beautifully constructed high vaulted brick ceiling and at one end of the cellar natural rock forms one of the walls, presumably because it was too hard to be removed. Like all good cellars the temperature remains constant winter and summer. At the top of the flight of steps that leads down to the cellar a colony of bats hangs from the beams watching those that pass underneath with considerable interest. The bats are greatly valued as they help to control the mosquitoes.

The Supporting Cast

GIVEN THE SCALE of their endeavours in the garden and on the buildings, it quickly became apparent to both Don and Lindsay that they were going to need some help. Early on they met an English couple, Chris and Gabby, who live nearby at Colle di Val d'Elsa and they enlisted their help with the garden in spring and autumn. It was the fact that they were willing to work, rather than their Englishness, which led to their involvement, as at that time no Italians were interested in working in the gardens at Venzano and the enthusiasm of the English pair made a refreshing change. The friendship is now long-established and it has worked well, but, with Don and Lindsay's blessing, Chris and Gabby have now branched out on their own. When the apartments were finally completed, Don and Lindsay needed look no further for help than their nearest neighbour, Grazia, who lives in a house just across the adjoining valley with her husband Fulvio and their young children. She acts as housekeeper for the apartments and the main house and also works in the nursery. Fulvio was an artist but gave up painting some time ago and now helps in the gardens. Grazia and Fulvio would love to work full time at Venzano, but there isn't the money available for this, as yet. Venzano's resident character is Franco who, before he retired, owned the Albana Restaurant in Mazzolla. Following his retirement his wife quickly tired of having him home all day and told him to visit Venzano "to see if the chaps had any work for him". In the interest of good neighbourliness and encouraging marital harmony, they asked Franco to take on the strimming of the grass in the car park. One day, he came to Don and Lindsay and said, "Why don't we make a vegetable garden?" They agreed to make one on a very overgrown area lower down the hill and in no time he had cleared half the hillside and established "his" vegetable garden which he visits twice daily.

Another important presence at Venzano is Domenica the cat, usually to be found not far from where Don or Lindsay are working. She has a strong sense of her decorative qualities and will arrange herself picturesquely, as if inviting them to consider placing a cat sculpture in the exact spot she has chosen. With the best will in the world her son Fatty could not be called picturesque – he has something of the gargoyle about him with his rotund body, battered face, shredded ears and missing tail! What he lacks in looks he makes up for in good nature, responding gratefully to any attention he is paid.

above (top): *Domenica is something of a poser, always finding a spot where she will draw favourable comments. She remains loftily aloof, spurning the attentions of those who pause to admire her.*

above (below): *Domenica's son Fatty could not be more different, but what he lacks in looks he makes up for in good nature, responding gratefully to any attention he is paid.*

opposite (left): *Franco is never happier than when he is hard at work with his strimmer or tending his vegetable garden at Venzano.*

opposite (centre): *Chris and Gabby provided much needed help in the early days at Venzano, but now work independently in the area.*

opposite (right): *Their neighbour Grazia maintains the apartments for them and works in the garden whenever time permits her to do so.*

opposite left: *Fulvio, Grazia's husband, with their dog Yorgo. Since starting to work seasonally at Venzano, Fulvio has discovered a latent talent as a plant propagator, sometimes succeeding with plants where Don and Lindsay have failed.*

red, all shown to perfection against the dark green of the bay hedges. Whatever the choice, the fragrance of the flowers will imprint this moment indelibly upon the memory.

Most first-time visitors to Venzano are surprised to see how green western Tuscany is in the spring. What will, after harvest, become a seemingly barren moonscape is richly verdant earlier in the year, more like Ireland than Italy. Looking southwards it is apparent that the landscape around Venzano is on a larger, less populated scale than eastern Tuscany where the hills are covered with olive groves or scrub woodland, a house perched on every one of them. In western Tuscany, the hills roll away to the horizon, with only the occasional building to be seen, and later exploration will reveal that many of these are uninhabited ruins. In such a vast panorama, it becomes impossible to judge the distance between one hill and another.

Looking away from the view, the eye focuses on the buildings of Venzano and its surrounding gardens. The warm golden stone walls and terracotta roof tiles are classically Tuscan and it is clear that these buildings have stood here for many

First Impressions

THE MOMENT YOU ARRIVE at Venzano, climbing from your car to stand and admire the magnificent panoramic view which is spread before you, you are enveloped by the heady clove-scent of carnations (*Dianthus*). Their siren call is irresistible and whatever your original intention, you will find yourself drawn to the Dianthus Garden. This, it has to be said, is no hardship, for its position is perfect, bordered on three sides by tall, immaculately trimmed bay hedges, and with its southern side opening onto a paved terrace which overlooks the rolling Tuscan hills. A strategically placed table and chairs invite you to sit down and enjoy this sublime moment; the only dilemma to be faced is whether to look outwards at the view or inwards to cushioned mounds of soft grey-green foliage topped with flowers in every shade from white, through pink, to deep

centuries. The lane continues its uneven way past the buildings, separating the south-facing gardens from the house and the apartments. These gardens are shielded from the lane by tall, carefully trimmed bay hedges, into which arches have been cut for access. An arch opposite the Dianthus Garden leads to a terrace and the entrance to one of the apartments. The terrace is planted with crimson trailing pelargoniums, rosemary and thyme and shaded by a vine-covered pergola. A second apartment adjoins this one with a raised terrace reached by a flight of stone steps. The wall flanking the steps is covered with a magnificent Cooper's Burmese rose, a mass of large, white single flowers of particular beauty (see page 22 and overleaf).

Opposite the apartment steps there is another archway in the bay hedge - this one leading to the Bulb Garden. The entrance is barred by an intriguingly low gate, so low that it is easily stepped over, but then this gate is not designed to exclude humans - it is a porcupine gate. These creatures are quite common in Tuscany and as bulbs are a favourite delicacy, the gate prevents the Bulb Garden from turning into a popular night-time rendezvous for hungry porcupines.

Further down the lane, past the Bulb Garden, a path leads off to the left down a gentle slope shaded by overhanging vines to the spring and the vegetable garden, both of which are tucked out of sight of the house and the lane. Opposite the path, on the other side of the lane, a couple of steps lead up to the Gravel Garden, the several entrances to the main house and also to the chapel.

The soil of Venzano (in the areas where it hasn't been worked for centuries) is a limestone clay-loam, although much more on the loam side. It is quite well-drained, if a little bit gooey, but any part of the garden which has been worked is wonderfully rich and very fertile. A testament to this fertility can be found in the Bulb Garden where some lilies will flower within a year of the seed being sown, instead of the two to three years normally expected. The bay hedging used throughout to divide the different gardens

opposite: Looking south across flowering thymes in the Dry Garden the hills roll away to the horizon under a cloudless blue sky.

left (above): Dianthus *'Earl of Essex' has attractively fringed petals.*
left (below): *Within the intimate confines of the bay-hedged Dianthus Garden the clove-scented flowers fill the air with their delicious fragrance while their soft colours, offset by the silver foliage, creates a subtle tapestry.*

has proved a great success. Its structural quality complements the hard landscaping and it also provides essential shelter for the plants from the cold north wind during the hard Tuscan winter. When the hedging was planted it was fed and watered for the first year but subsequently has needed no attention other than regular trimming to keep its shape.

The presence, and occasional absence, of water is a central consideration in the gardens at Venzano. The property has been connected to the town water supply for the last five years but this is purely for domestic use and not for the gardens, which nonetheless need watering. On the whole, the spring is reliable but in a very long hot summer it will get low, especially when Franco assiduously waters the vegetable garden. Apart from the plants in pots, Don and Lindsay water very little, preferring the plants to toughen up to the prevailing conditions. Even when a garden is newly planted it is only watered four or five times to

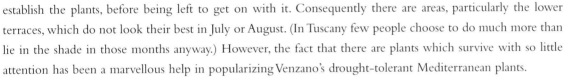

establish the plants, before being left to get on with it. Consequently there are areas, particularly the lower terraces, which do not look their best in July or August. (In Tuscany few people choose to do much more than lie in the shade in those months anyway.) However, the fact that there are plants which survive with so little attention has been a marvellous help in popularizing Venzano's drought-tolerant Mediterranean plants.

Don's love of both formal and cottage gardens has determined the style of the gardens at Venzano. Somehow the gardens here bridge the gap between formality and informality, combining the best of both. There is a formality to the structure, but within it you will find the glorious profusion and informality of a cottage garden. This underlying structure has been carefully planned and much of it now implemented, but there is also a welcome spontaneity that arises in response to a need for planting space – Don cannot bear to keep stock plants in pots. As a result, a new bed is occasionally developed with no real reference to the original plans and the garden just grows accordingly.

Like all working gardens, there is no moment of perfection at Venzano – there are always weedy corners that have been left because more urgent work beckons, and even in Tuscany the weather is unpredictable and plants preform earlier or later than expected. Although they sometimes wish that they were more on top of things, neither Don nor Lindsay are trying to produce manicured perfection. They like to allow plants to grow as they please and enjoy the way many of them self-seed freely. In fact, they revel in the unexpected results when plants cross-fertilize to produce new and interesting varieties.

In retrospect, Don and Lindsay realize that the knowledge and experience they brought with them from Herefordshire has not been particularly useful – gardening here is so totally different that they have had to discount much of what they knew and start again. Originally they had planned to specialize in old roses and pinks but these have not been the easiest plants to grow in this climate and are now only a small part of the nursery's stock, which has a much more Mediterranean flavour.

opposite: *The huge, single white flower of the Cooper's Burmese rose only has the faintest of scents but you can forgive it this shortcoming given its perfect beauty.*
above: *A split-open seed-head of* Paeonia mascula *reveals glossy black fruit.*

The Seasons

JUST AS THE ROOFLINE of Venzano's buildings melds together many different levels, reflecting the gradual growth of the ancient monastery, so the terraces surrounding the house reveal the evolution of the various gardens. Since their arrival Don and Lindsay have renovated existing terraces and developed some of their own so that the cultivated area has gradually expanded around the south, east and west of the hilltop site. In general, the slopes are gentle and one garden leads into another via shallow flights of steps, although occasionally a high wall separates them as it does between one part the Courtyard and the Upper Garden. Although the gardens do not cover a large area (no more than a couple of acres at the most), this frequent change of level creates the impression of a much larger space, and with most of the gardens hidden from one another by terrace walls and high bay hedges, a walk around the garden is a constant journey of discovery.

Spring

THE WARM, WET WEATHER which is normal at this time of year results in a rich green landscape where plants grow at an astonishing rate. This is also true of Venzano where it becomes impossible to keep pace with the work in the garden. Now is the time to bring out all the tender plants from their winter quarters in the barn and the other outbuildings, to sow seeds, and pot them on as they germinate with unseemly haste, to trim, to train, to feed and generally make the most of this, the kindest of seasons.

The weather in Tuscany is usually warm at this time of year, but very variable, and it moves across the landscape at an astonishing pace – one moment there is bright, hot sunshine, the next moment clouds bubble up, and it pours with rain, or a fierce wind starts to blow and the temperature drops dramatically. Most afternoons a storm threatens, with thunder rumbling around the surrounding hills and distant flashes of lightning, but more often than not these storms miss Venzano itself and the late afternoon sky clears to give a golden evening. This is a time of year when Venzano is at its best with drifts of flowers in every part of the garden, but especially the Grey Garden, which defies its name with a spectacular display in many shades of blue, set off by a small number of plants that provide a yellow accent.

opposite: *The wild sweet pea flowering in the Bulb Garden. It re-appears annually without any help from Venzano's gardeners.*

Swallows, like feathered guided missiles, hurtle in and out of doorways at breathtaking speed as they work on rebuilding their nests and raising a new brood. Domenica, the cat, loathes them with a passion and will often steal out of the byre door, flattening herself against the ground, confident of her invisibility, as she stalks them. They think otherwise and launch a concerted attack, dive-bombing her en masse until she loses her nerve and slinks back indoors. During the day the constant twittering conversation of the swallows mingles with the calls of other birds, both familiar and unfamiliar, to create a complex symphony of birdsong.

When Don and Lindsay first arrived at Venzano the bird population was almost non-existent, but over the years many have taken up residence, thanks in part to the safe haven offered to them and also to a growing environmental awareness in Italy. Bee-eaters were hardly ever seen in the early years, but since Venzano has now become a bee-friendly zone, they visit daily through spring and summer. Workers in the garden are endlessly diverted by the sight of these charming birds flying by with bumble-bees firmly clamped in their beaks.

Of all the birds that charm and delight Don and Lindsay and their guests, the nightingales are unrivalled. Five pairs nest regularly in thickets around the gardens and through spring and

early summer the hauntingly beautiful song makes the sweetest of lullabies as Venzano's residents drift off to sleep. The nightingales arrive in March but remain discreetly silent until they start mating and nesting, whereupon they start singing. Some less romantically minded guests have even complained that they have been kept awake by them. However, to those of us used to the endless noise pollution of the 20th century, it is a revelation to be in a place where the loudest noises are birdsong, the buzz of insects, the scutter of lizards and the raucous croak of a bullfrog as he does his wooing in the pond in the courtyard. Ears that are used to blocking out background noise become sensitive to the quietest of sounds – the rustle of the wind among the plants, the creak of sun-warmed wood, the gentle trickle of water into the pond and the flutter of bats' wings in the evening air.

The result of this peaceful and tranquil atmosphere is that many people speak in low voices and whispers as they walk around the garden. Not so, however, the more exuberant Italians who often arrive in large family groups, chattering away like a flock of starlings. Often one of the party is so moved by Venzano that he or she finds it essential to call a friend on the mobile phone to describe the wonders of the *bel giardino*. Their enthusiasm is infectious, in particular their excited reaction to the Cooper's Burmese rose. They all want their own version of this rose but propagation problems make this an unlikely event.

opposite: *All hands are enlisted at this time of year to help with the endless round of seed-sowing and potting on.*

left: *Looking across at the house from a terrace in the Dry Garden the wisteria-like white flowers of the acacia trees make a magnificent display against a stormy sky.*

Summer

I N HIGH SUMMER, when the surrounding landscape is pre-dominantly earth-toned, even Venzano's gardens look dusty and bleached out. Fresh green foliage and colourful flowers survive in few places other than under the trees in the Gravel Garden and in the shade of the pergolas where the visitor can still find the lushness of an oasis. Elsewhere, the dianthus have finished flowering and the roses are taking a rest, but what is lacking in colour is made up for in fragrance. Walking around Venzano at this time of year the air is heavy with the scent of the many aromatic herbs that are grown in the gardens. Sages, savory, thyme and rosemary mingle with the more exotic fragrances of patchouli and vetiver in the Gravel Garden. The path beneath the pergola in the Bulb Garden is lined with many varieties of scented pelargonium that variously release the perfume of attar of roses, camphor, orange, lemon and sandalwood as you pass by.

Rare jasmines, clustered in pots next to the kitchen door, bear small but intensely fragrant flowers, the perfume of which blends with nearby lemon and orange blossom and in the cool of the pergola which runs along the length of the house you may, if you are very lucky, witness the night-flowering of an extraordinarily beautiful and fragrant cactus, *Epiphyllum oxypetalum*.

Whilst most of nature has entered a quiet, somnolent phase, the reverse is true of Venzano's insect life. There is the constant, insistent buzz of the cicadas from dawn to dusk, large shiny flying beetles drone by intermittently and mosquito netting becomes essential at night or sleep will be disturbed by the predatory whine of mosquitoes. Flies are a persistent nuisance in the kitchen but, following an old Tuscan tradition, Don and Lindsay put scented pelargonium leaves on the table at mealtimes to repel them. Outdoors, fortunately, the scorpions keep to themselves in

left: *As summer progresses the meadows and surrounding landscape take on the golden hues typical of Tuscany.*

centre: *At Venzano the scent of jasmine mingles with aromatic herbs on the evening air.*

right: *Harvest in, caterpillar tractors plough the surrounding fields ready for the next crop.*

crevices between rocks and under piles of bricks, but the scuttering of lizards as they scrabble through dry foliage can alarm those of a nervous disposition. Snakes are rarely seen at Venzano. In the twelve years Don and Lindsay have been there, Don has had only one close encounter with a viper, which was sunbathing curled around a dianthus plant from which he was about to take cuttings. This is the only poisonous snake in Tuscany; all the others are totally harmless, including the very beautiful bronze-coloured Aesculapian snake which is immortalized in the traditional doctor's symbol.

Although most plants are not now growing as actively in the arid heat, the pace of work does not let up. It is essential to water all the potted plants twice daily in very hot weather and as most of this is done by hand the task can occupy the majority of the day, so Don, Lindsay and their various helpers are seldom seen around the garden without a watering can in hand.

In general, the summer gardens of Venzano are best appreciated early in the morning, before the sun becomes too strong, or in the relative cool of the evening, otherwise the visitor, like the plants, will struggle not to wilt in the heat. Most retreat indoors where the thick walls and tiled floors keep the interiors cool and comfortable, and an afternoon siesta is a sensible choice. But whatever the time of day, the pace is always gentler as everyone tries to conserve their energy as best they can.

Autumn

D URING AUTUMN the banks of the lane leading to Venzano are a mass of wild clematis, blackberries and fennel, and tall spires of blue-flowered chicory. From the fields above, olives hang over the roadway, heavy with half-ripened fruit. Further down the lane past the house, tendrils of *Smilax* scramble over and through the undergrowth; the sweet scent of their flowers fills the air and the clusters of jewel-bright berries change from red to black as they ripen.

The Dianthus Garden has been shorn of its summer flowers and foliage and the plants cling neatly to their beds. In the middle, Domenica the cat takes a dust bath and lures passers-by to tickle her snow-white tummy. A pretty, lilac pink *Centranthus* and white rosemaries bring colour to an almost monochromatic scene of steely-grey gravel, soft grey tufa-rock and blue-grey dianthus foliage.

Everywhere, lily stems make bold statements with their swollen seedpods. In the Dianthus Garden they appear architectural, swaying in unison in a light breeze and in the Bulb Garden self-sown "volunteers" bar paths and steps wherever they have chosen to grow. The white perfection of a solitary *Lilium formosanum* flower defies autumn in an unseasonal display.

The self-seeded 'marvel of Peru' *(Mirabilis jalapa)* brightens path edges and verges with flowers in a range of colours from pale primrose through yellow and orange to shocking pink. The pomegranate tree hangs heavy with fruit, as does the persimmon with its perfect, glowing golden orbs. The jube-jube tree is festooned with small circular red brown fruit – much less spectacular than the other seasonal fruit but with an interesting and elusive flavour.

Along the pergola in the Bulb Garden the late-ripening pointed fruit of cornicella grapes hang from the vines. The end of each fruit looks as if it has been placed in a pencil sharpener, and the effect of the bunches is most curious. Beneath the vines, Venzano's collection of aromatic pelargoniums is still in flower, including a creamy-yellow flowered trailing pelargonium of particularly subtle and unusual beauty.

Leading down to the spring, the wall has been lined by Franco with some of his crop of pumpkins; in the evening sunlight they glow like benevolent sentinels guarding the pathway. At this time of year the water level of the spring is often very low, allowing you to look right down the carved passageway into the hillside. Those brave enough – it feels like going back in time to the days when the Etruscans collected their water here – can walk down the tunnel and see how it branches as it leads back into the hillside. The low autumn sunlight illuminates the passageway at the end of the day, bathing the spring in golden light and giving the place a magical and powerful atmosphere.

right: *The evening light gives Franco's tomatoes a jewel-like appearance. The strange shape of the fruit is characteristic of 'Mostro de Firenze', which is a local Tuscan variety much favoured by Franco.*

In Franco's vegetable garden, autumn is showing its effects – the tomatoes are nearly over, the pumpkins, marrows, gourds and melons are fully expanded and the autumn and winter vegetables are well established. Recent depredations by the porcupines mean that most of the melons have been eaten by them just as they reached perfection, so time will have to be taken to patch and repair the fence. Until there is some proper autumn rain to top up the spring, the frequent water shortages make it difficult to keep the garden growing the way Franco would really like.

At this time of year the calm of Venzano is disturbed by the distant pop-pop of the hunters' guns or the occasional, more disturbing, crack of a rifle. The hunters make noisy progress across the fields and through the

woodland, shouting and whistling, accompanied by the excited
barking of their dogs. With the racket they make, anything worth
shooting presumably makes a quick exit to the other side of
Tuscany. Although, in theory at least, the netting and shooting of
songbirds is no longer allowed in Italy, hunters remain a wild
bunch and the law is difficult to enforce, so Tuscan birdlife,
unfortunately, is likely to be at considerable risk beyond Venzano's
boundaries for the foreseeable future.

Winter

V ENZANO IS CLOSED to visitors, both to the gardens and
the apartments, from mid-December until mid-February.
This is a private time for Don and Lindsay, when they can re-charge
their batteries and start to make new plans for the garden and its
planting in the coming year.

THE GARDENS

Divided into compartments, the gardens at Venzano each have their own special planting or function, be it for bulbs or vegetables, or even for individual plants, such as carnations in the Dianthus Garden. Predominant in the planting, of course, is the accent on scent.

key to colour

Existing gardens

Incomplete gardens

apartment 3

2

3

apartment 1

apartment 2

4

7

6

5

8

ANO

10

JUST AS A FINE PERFUME is made by blending many different aromatic ingredients, so the scent that hangs in the air at Venzano is an amalgam of thousands of fragrant plants. The overall impression is of a resinous, woody scent, but as you move around the gardens it constantly changes, sometimes subtly, sometimes dramatically, depending on what is in flower, the time of year and the time of day. Early in the day and early in the year, the citrus-like, grassy aromas are most evident amongst the herbs in the Gravel Garden, a little later on and it is the delicious clove-scent of the Dianthus Garden which will imprint itself on your memory. As spring turns to summer, the roses and lavender in the Upper Garden and Gravel Garden take centre stage during daylight hours, followed by the haunting fragrance of lilies on the evening air in the Bulb Garden. As your senses become attuned to Venzano it is not just the peace and beauty which become apparent, it is also the tapestry of perfumes which constantly surround and envelop you in these gardens.

The Barn Garden

ON THE SOUTH SIDE of the lane as it widens on its approach to Venzano, there is a simple rectangular stone barn. It is used for over-wintering the more delicate plants and as a storage place for bulbs, tubers and seeds. There are tentative plans to convert it into another apartment, but Don and Lindsay feel that the balance is just right at the moment and another apartment might prove to be one too many, so it is likely to remain a barn for the foreseeable future.

Outside the main doors of the barn there is a stone terrace and a simple pergola which they lovingly constructed to support four 'Gloire de Dijon' roses which were bought specifically for this spot, and duly planted in carefully enriched soil, watered, fed and pampered. To Don and Lindsay's horror three out of the four

of them have turned out to be double vermilion-red roses in spite of the labels stating that they were 'Gloire de Dijon'. Mortified that anyone might think that they had actually chosen to plant these brash-coloured roses, Don was not surprised when a visiting friend gasped, "Oh my God" on setting eyes on them. "We know", said Don, "They are going to go". "No", she said, "My dears, you mustn't. I love them. These are the classic *contadino* red rose." The contadino rose is the one that was traditionally planted by the self-sufficient Tuscan small-holders, known as *contadini,* to mingle amongst the vines on their pergolas. Vigorous and very colourful, it is not at all subtle. Don's comment in reply was that his friend had no taste! Anyway, *contadini* or not, Don is determined that these roses have to go. They will be cut back, dug up and presented to the friend who so admired them. In their place, because you cannot replant roses where other roses have grown without allowing the soil a four-year rest, Don and Lindsay are planning to plant a white and a blue wisteria, and another *contadini* favourite – the strawberry grape (*Vitis* 'Fragola'). They already have one of these vines; which never gets mildew and the fruit stays on the vine in good condition long after any other variety.

Theoretically, they are quite rare because no-one is supposed to sell them any more. Despite the fact that the Italians have been making a fine wine called *fragolino* from the strawberry grape for the last hundred and twenty years, it is now prohibited to make home-made wine from it because it can have a very high wood-alcohol content, with serious consequences to health.

left: *The "flower of the west wind"* (Zephyranthus candida) *blooms after the first rains of the autumn.*
below: *The recently planted Tuscan cypresses have surprised Don and Lindsay with their speed of growth.*

In autumn, the gravel at the edge of the terrace is carpeted with the "flower of the west wind" *(Zephyranthus candida)* with its pretty crocus-like white flowers. It is completely dormant in summer but as soon as the autumn rains arrive, it comes into flower. The bulbs were previously planted against the walls of the house where the porcupines treated them as a tasty snack, but they haven't as yet found them in their new position.

Between the barn and the lane there is, somewhat surprisingly, a sub-tropical camphor laurel *(Cinnamomum camphora)* which is growing well in spite of being in the path of the north wind. It is a tree that has naturalized in the temperate regions of Australia and the wonderful fragrance of the leaves reminds Don of childhood trips when he made camp-fires from the branches. The reason for its slightly strange position is that Don and Lindsay find it hard to make a decision on where to plant such permanent fixtures, often disagreeing on the best position, until Don finally takes it upon himself to plant it where he chooses!

Behind the camphor laurel, next to the lane, Don has planted a row of classic Tuscan cypresses which are growing at an astonishing rate, confounding the myth that they are slow to grow. When people see 400- year-old specimens in Medici villas they presume that this indicates slow growth, but this has certainly not proved to be the case at Venzano.

The Grey Garden

THE GREY GARDEN, located between the Barn Garden and the Dianthus Garden, has been the cause of many "discussions" between Don and Lindsay. Its development came about because Don had become fed up with the messy area adjoining the car park, so they set to and constructed a new area of terrace (much more professional than their earliest efforts which are about to fall down). The walls of the terrace are built with stone from their own quarry – an enormous raft of bedrock discovered under a patch of rough grass when they were weeding out convolvulus and bindweed. Initially, it was quite easy to break off the pieces but now it has become increasingly difficult so the development of this area of garden has ground to a halt. While the weathered stone is quite easy to work, the stone which has been covered by soil is much harder, especially as no machines are used to cut it. They rely instead on Don's knowledge of geology, together with brute strength and simple tools, to break the stone following natural cracks.

Don and Lindsay's dry stone walls are a feature at Venzano, and their styles of dry-stone walling are markedly different. According to Lindsay, this is because Don helps himself to the best stones for his section. But according to Don, it is because his walls are inspired by Zimbabwean and medieval Roman styles (he likes to incorporate tiles in his) while Lindsay favours an Etruscan style. The result is walls that undergo a sudden change of style half-way along. Fortunately the effect is more quirky than jarring because the natural materials go together so well.

Blending harmoniously with the natural stone of the walls, the paths, steps and some border edges are made up of tufa blocks. Although very regular when freshly laid, the porous nature of the rock means that it weathers down beautifully, and crevices and dips open up where herbs can seed themselves and mosses can take hold. The colour of the tufa quickly mellows amd although it resembles a type of breeze-block initially, time gradually reveals its organic origins.

The architecture of the Grey Garden has been planned to incorporate plants that have been selected for shape and form to ensure that the borders are interesting during the long, non-flowering gap in Tuscany from June to September. In time, the pyramid-shaped olives which punctuate the borders will develop into wonderfully architectural trees; meanwhile, wild artichokes have been planted below them, their jagged foliage, a beautiful blue-grey during the summer. There is also a deliciously scented herbaceous honeysuckle *(Lonicera implexa)* which is native to the area and thrives on the hot dry, serpentine slopes in the volcanic region just to the south of Venzano. It is more of a shrub than a climber, although it will clamber through bushes, and in the extreme heat of summer, its oval leaves become like leather.

Don has found a place here for one of his favourite roses *(Rosa hemisphaerica)* whose totally double flowers form a spherical sulphur-yellow ball. Nearby there is a very, very old variety of single China rose with beautiful deep-red flowers and wonderful pointed buds given to them by their friend, Joan Tesei, who got her original plant from Texas! Their own Venzano lavender 'June Ellen' (named after Don's mother) is also included in the planting. Although it is not reliably hardy, it grows quickly from cuttings and is so lovely that it is worth treating

opposite: *Elegant flower spikes of* Lavandula dentata *'Royal Crown' border tufa steps leading down from the Grey Garden.*
above (top): *Looking westwards across the Grey Garden.*
above: *The attractive silvery leaves of* Tanacetum densum.

left (top): *Shrubby germander* (Teucrium fruticans) *with its silvery grey aromatic leaves and bright blue flowers loves the hot dry conditions of the Grey Garden.*

left (centre): *Nepeta nepetoides, a member of the catmint family, which flowers profusely from late spring through to early summer.*

left (below): *The Venzano form of* Linum narbonense *is a deep, almost iridescent, rich blue.*

opposite: *The softly coloured pendant bells of the spring-flowering* Nectaroscordum siculum.

as an annual and replanting when it doesn't make it through the winter. A particularly fine prostrate rosemary, 'Gethsemane' (from where it originated), tumbles over the terrace walls. It is so smothered with soft blue flowers that the foliage is barely visible. In amongst these architectural plants there are also trial plants which are being checked to see if they are going to be worth propagating for sale in the nursery.

There is still work to be done before the Grey Garden is complete, and a further terrace below the existing border will double the planting area and give access to the olive grove below, while the inclusion of a bay hedge to the north should make these the most protected borders at Venzano. Don hopes it will be sufficiently sheltered to grow silver-leaved echiums. Last year one was doing really well until about three weeks before flowering, when it was literally blown out of the border and died. Currently Don is taking no chances and keeps them in the poly tunnel.

There are times of year, especially spring, when the Grey Garden defies its name and is full of colour, in soft shades of blue and yellow. Creamy yellow Californian poppies and bright yellow phlomis jostle with blue-flowered cat-mints, salvias and flax, a counterpoint to the textures and silvery foliage. As the most recent garden to be developed, it has benefited from the expertise that Don has acquired over the years and the planting here is both accomplished and refined.

The Courtyard

THE COURTYARD WAS predominantly functional until recently, but now – since it has been tidied and made more decorative – the beauty of its proportions are properly revealed. An elegant stone sink, uncovered after being abandoned many years ago, now graces the wall flanking the steps that lead to the Upper Garden. Passionflower and jasmine climb the wall and variegated pelargoniums decorate the sink. Underneath it, the broad-leaves of *Jaborosa integrifolia,* punctuated with starry white flowers, create a soft margin against the stone wall and the blossom perfumes the evening air. Don thought it was a tropical rarity but has since found it to be hardy to -15°C (5°F), invasive, and able to grow practically anywhere!

Adjoining the steps is the *vasca* (formal pond) where water-lilies and lotus bloom throughout the summer. Water splashes gently onto the surface of the pond from a simple spout in the wall, a gentle sound which adds to the tranquillity of the spot and encourages you to sit and imagine the generations of inhabitants who have enjoyed this place. At the far end of the pool, the exotic trumpet flowers of huge *Brugmansia* (formerly *Datura*) plants overhang the water while the wall above is planted mainly with caper berries, with their soft pink flowers.

The construction of the pool was an ongoing project which was suddenly accelerated into hurried completion for a friend's wedding party to be held in the courtyard. As soon as the pond was filled, the water became infested with mosquito larvae and Don had to trawl the pet shops of three towns to acquire nine goldfish. There are now hundreds and the ever-expanding population ensures that mosquitoes get no chance to breed.

At the south end of the courtyard, a blue-and-white flowered wisteria climbs a stone pillar in readiness for the day when there is time to construct a pergola. Opposite the wisteria, large wooden doors conceal a smaller courtyard which contains the wood store and some wonderfully rustic cold-frames. There are plans to turn this area into a secret garden at some point, but the walls are in ruins and other parts of the garden have prior claims for attention. Wintersweet *(Chimonanthus praecox)* is growing nearby. When it is in flower, early in the year, the scent is so strong that it carries to the far side of the building.

opposite (top):
The Vasca (formal pond) creates a focal point in the Courtyard at the bottom of the flight of steps leading to the Upper Garden.

opposite (below):
The pure perfection of a waterlily bloom is reflected in the clear water of the Vasca.

left: *The sound of water splashing into the pond is pleasantly refreshing, especially in the stifling heat of summer. Don and Lindsay have resisted using an ornate fountainhead, opting instead for a simple semi-circular runnel.*

The Upper Garden

left: *Framed by the view to the south, and one of Venzano's buildings, a poppy has self-seeded on a wall.*

opposite: *In the Upper Garden dark red roses and olives grow almost level with the rooftops that surround the Courtyard.*

IF YOU CLIMB THE STEPS next to the pond in the courtyard, you reach the Upper Garden with its view over the rooftops of Venzano - the undulating tiles and the many angles of the different roofs reveal the evolving history of the buildings far more clearly than can be observed from ground level. At one stage, when they were doing restoration work, Don and Lindsay found a Roman roof tile of exactly the same shape as modern tiles, but double the thickness.

A gravel path bordered by olive trees leads to one of the apartments, which in earlier times served as a sheep pen and also as a priest's house. Now it is the most tucked away of the apartments with a secluded terrace enclosed by fragrant climbing roses. Beyond the path, box-edged beds are planted with the old roses in which Don and Lindsay had planned to specialize until the climate dictated otherwise. A few have done well, some struggle on valiantly and the rest have succumbed. In the early days, they also collected cuttings from old moss roses growing on the roadside, but eventually gave up doing this because it drove Don mad to think that he would never be able to accurately identify the different varieties.

Quite early on in the process of restoring the terraces and laying the paths around the Upper Garden, they disturbed a monks' burial ground. To everyone's distress, the digger unexpectedly uncovered a mass of skeletons, laid out in orderly fashion. To atone for this disruption, a friend who was visiting lit candles around the garden and they decided to rebury the skeletons. Don, who collected the remains together, was fascinated to notice that all the teeth in the skulls were quite perfect. They had some difficulty deciding where to rebury the remains. Don's suggestion of a site under the 'Rambling Rector' rose was deemed irreverent, but they finally found a quiet place, unlikely to be disturbed by further earthworks.

A major feature of the Upper Garden is the terracing, and until quite recently Don had a cherished pile of stones here which he was saving to complete a dry stone wall along the terrace. However, when the builders were strengthening the foundations of the tall rear wall that keeps the house from tumbling into the valley below, they commandeered the pile and used all Don's precious stones in the foundations, including the fine, hand-worked corner ones, much to his chagrin.

The Dianthus Garden

THE DIANTHUS GARDEN was one of the first areas to be laid out when Don and Lindsay arrived at Venzano, but their early efforts ended in disaster. After growing dianthus in England and struggling to prevent them rotting off during the winter, they decided to give the plants the best possible start in their new Tuscan garden by ensuring that the newly created raised beds had excellent drainage, filling them with compost liberally mixed with copious quantities of limestone rubble and grit. With the garden laid out to their satisfaction, complete with stone raised beds, gravel paths and newly planted bay hedges, they were ready to begin planting. On a return visit to England. Don called on their old friend Sophie Hughes, holder of the National Dianthus Collection in Herefordshire,

opposite: The bay hedges and the topiary rosemary bushes provide a perfect formal framework within which the the dianthus have an informal charm.

above: *The column topped with a stone ball in the Dianthus Garden was intended to be a sundial, but an exorbitantly high quotation for the sundial determined them on a simpler solution.*

hoping that she could be persuaded to sell them some cuttings. Sophie was delighted to help and, with the generosity of spirit which characterizes true gardeners, she presented a delighted Don with the cuttings as a gift. Many of them were from treasured old varieties and he believed that they would give the Dianthus Garden a brilliant start.

Unfortunately the superb drainage in the raised beds proved to be too much of a good thing. The consequence was that their precious plants began to shrivel and die. Gradually it dawned on them what they had done. They had created a desert! In those early days when so many other activities demanded their attention, there simply wasn't time to nurse the plants through the summer heat and they lost many which were great favourites, including the double-

right: Dianthus 'Kandahar' *is one of Don's favourites, and is particularly richly scented.*

ringed varieties that Don considered to be the finest in the collection. Fortunately, those which survived have gone from strength to strength, especially after their environment was adapted to make it less hostile. Don remains enduringly grateful to Sophie for her generosity and, when her own collection was ravaged by disease, he was delighted to be able to repay her by sending her cuttings.

In the country areas of Italy, dianthus plants are seldom valued for their flowers; it is the leaves that count, as they are used as an emetic feed for snails, to cleanse them for the table. Indeed, every country vegetable garden has a patch of dianthus in the corner. It was just such a patch which provided Don and Lindsay with one of their loveliest dianthus. Their friend Jane had found a particularly lovely clump of pinks in her newly acquired garden which she showed to Don, who was enchanted by their frilly white flowers and fine fragrance. To mark Jane's contribution to his collection, Don decided to christen the plant 'Jane's White Frilly'. When she heard the name she was extremely offended, assuming Don was referring to her underwear. Don responded by explaining that she was in good company, because there is a pink variety called 'Frank's Frilly', but the "Frilly" reference had more to do with the petal shape than intimate apparel!

The dianthus beds are given height and structure by the inclusion of clipped rosemary. This is thought of as a very common plant by the Italians, akin to a weed, but Don and Lindsay have succeeded in persuading them otherwise by introducing them to its many varieties. 'Israeli Commercial' has been a particular success. Similar to *Rosmarinus pyramidalis* but with more fleshy leaves, it has responded well to being trimmed into ball and box shapes, thus making ideal topiary for this region.

There are plans to relocate the Dianthus Garden as it has not proved to be as successful as they had hoped, and the dianthus plants will be replaced by aromatic herbs. The new Dianthus Garden will be sited in front of the barn to ensure that their scent still greets visitors upon arrival.

above: Dianthus *'Allspice'*

left: Dianthus damasco

73

The Bulb Garden

LIKE THE DIANTHUS GARDEN, the Bulb Garden is hidden from the lane and sheltered from northerly winds by a tall bay hedge. To gain entry you must open or step over the "porcupine gate" which protects the bulbs from night-time raiders. A rustic pergola leads visitors down the length of the garden to the edge of the terrace where there is a view to rival that seen from the Dianthus Garden. Flanking the central pergola are seed beds where spring bulbs and lilies are raised each year in conditions of such suitability that they grow like weeds. This is a garden which is at its best in the spring or early summer when the narcissus, species tulip and lilies are accompanied by rich red paeonies, lavender and rosemary. They grow twelve species of narcissus of which three are native to the Mediterranean; they start flowering in November and continue all through the winter. The paeonies are Greek and utterly drought resistant - the same variety can be found growing on Mount Olympus. Paeonies are often thought of as native to China alone, but there are approximately twelve that are native

opposite (left): The day lily (Hemerocalllis flava) is not a true lily, despite its appearance.

above: In the spring, clusters of star of Bethlehem (Orni-thogalum nutans) emerge.

following spread: The Bulb Garden in spring.

to southern Europe, all of which are deliciously scented. At Venzano, they are grown from seed and flower in about four years.

The lilies here are all grown from seed and flower from May through to September, unlike the usual Dutch hybrids which all flower at the same time. Don is particularly proud of the fact that he has managed to instill into Italian gardeners a new appreciation of white lilies. They tended to think of them as funereal, but he is slowly persuading them to grow white lilies as well.

Later in the year, the Bulb Garden tends to become quite scruffy since only limited weeding is possible to avoid uprooting the precious young bulbils. Yet among the nodding seedheads and dusty foliage there are still solitary treasures – the pure white trumpet of a late-flowering *Lilium formosanum,* an autumn-flowering narcissus and the scented pelargoniums which spend the summer in the shade of the pergola. No month of the year is barren of flowers in the Bulb Garden – even in winter the "tazetta" narcissus will be in bloom.

The Vine Walk and the Ancient Spring

CONTINUE DOWN THE LANE past the Bulb Garden and you will come to the vine-shaded path leading to the spring. The vines which straddle it are 200 to 300 years old. Because of Venzano's isolation they survived the devastating *Phylloxera* epidemic that wiped out most of Europe's vineyards, but sadly, in spite of their venerable pedigree, they do not make a drinkable wine. Perhaps their very age is a factor!

The path turns a corner against the end wall of the Bulb Garden, and there, tucked into the hillside, is the spring. There is little doubt that this is the reason why Venzano has been in habitation for so long. When Don and Lindsay first came here it was invisible, totally obscured by an extensive patch of brambles. Wary of being duped, they insisted on taking a look before agreeing to the purchase; so the diminutive Sicilian owner and his family proceeded to hack an extremely low tunnel through which Don and Lindsay duly scrabbled on hands and knees, with some difficulty, to view their precious water supply for the first time – clean, clear and sweet in spite of its long concealment.

At first glance the ancient spring appears to consist of nothing more than a small medieval arch behind which there is a long pool of water. Closer inspection reveals a major work of engineering thought to be Etruscan in origin. Its full extent becomes apparent when the sun sinks low in the sky during spring and autumn and illuminates the archway, revealing a carved passageway stretching back into the hill for an estimated 30m (33yds). Extraordinarily, and surely not by accident, the sun sets directly opposite the entrance at the vernal and autumnal equinox. How the Etruscans could have excavated the tunnel is an unresolved mystery, especially as it narrows down progressively the further it recedes into the hillside. Some of the tunnel is constructed of blockwork and some carved from the hillside itself, and off to either side there are unseen galleries – six according to Franco, who knows an old local who used to go down into the spring to help clean it out. Don suspects that the present falling water level may relate to the fact that they haven't cleaned out these galleries since they arrived at Venzano. They are so narrow that he is reluctant to embark on this until such time as it proves absolutely essential. At times when the water level is low it becomes possible to see the earlier structures within the spring

that would have formed the original water collection system and at these times access also becomes somewhat easier. Not long ago one of Don's godsons who was staying at Venzano decided to take a closer look. He ventured into the tunnel, lying on a lilo, determined to explore its dark interior. Within a few minutes he fell off and emerged frozen and somewhat spooked. The ancient spring does not give up its secrets lightly.

Its water is pure and refreshing and was their sole supply for the first three years and continues to be a favourite stopping-off place for thirsty locals. A film of gypsum (alabaster powder) floats on the surface under which it is crystal clear. Curiously, there are times when the gypsum film disappears and then reappears – this is caused by the water temperature fluctuating – when the temperature rises the gypsum dissolves in the water only to precipitate again as the water cools. Anyone approaching the ancient spring causes consternation amongst the frog population who plop noisily into the water and conceal themselves on the floor of the spring. For some years there was also a resident fish, a river fish deposited there by persons unknown, which was almost albino from the low light conditions, but it eventually died – of loneliness, according to Don.

A huge, impossibly heavy, and wonderfully weathered stone bowl of indeterminate age stands sentinel next to the spring, its origins a mystery, although Don thinks it may have been an enormous mortar which was used with a pestle of similar scale to crush Venzano's olives. Besides the bowl a runnel carved through the ledge of the pool guides excess water away in times of plenty. An overflow originally channeled water under the path through an elegant system of old terracotta piping to a stone cistern and an area lower down the slopes where there are the remains of low retaining walls. The soil here is dark and fertile indicating that this was probably the location of the monastery gardens. Unfortunately, the neighbouring farmers have bulldozed away most of the walls, and the remains of the irrigation system which fed the beds.

opposite (left):
The Vine Walk leads down to the ancient spring and the Vegetable Garden.

opposite (right):
Turn the corner of the path and the previously hidden spring comes into view.

above (left):
The present stonework surrounding the spring dates back to the time the ancient monastery was established.

above (right):
Maidenhair ferns grow above the crystal clear waters of the spring.

The Vegetable Garden

TUCKED BELOW THE SPRING is the Vegetable Garden – on two accounts this is a felicitous location. Firstly, it benefits from plenty of ground water supplied from the spring and, secondly, it is sufficiently removed from the rest of the garden to ensure that Franco's more "rustic" aesthetic does not clash with the formality of the other areas. Empty plastic bottles rattle on bean poles or swing from lengths of string, and plastic flaps in the wind to deter marauding birds. Dilapidated wire-netting marks the garden's margins and creates an ineffective barrier against the porcupines which regularly broach the defences to plunder the melon patch, much to Franco's frustration and fury.

Nevertheless, in spite of these unwelcome predators, the garden is hugely productive and completely organic as Franco, mostly from an unwillingness to spend money, will not use any sprays. Like most Italian country dwellers, he plants strictly by the phases of the moon, with vegetables that carry their crops above ground planted on the waxing moon and those that crop below ground planted on the waning moon. Don and Lindsay now regularly deal with vast gluts brought on by Franco's

above: *A vast pumpkin and a couple of tomatoes rest on a rock, waiting to be taken to the house.*

left: *Franco's Vegetable Garden may look higgledy-piggledy, but it is very productive.*

no-holds-barred style of gardening. No sooner have they dealt with the European zuccini mountain than they are on to the cucumber glut and the more welcome bountiful harvest of wonderful tomatoes called 'Mostro di Firenze'. These are twice the size of beefsteak tomatoes and unbelievably gnarled and misshapen in appearance, but with a stunning flavour, particularly as the soil at Venzano is slightly salty, so the tomatoes grow ready salted! During much of the summer, these tomatoes are a staple food, served simply with oil and basil or chopped to accompany pasta.

Franco has a particular penchant for pumpkins and grows six or eight varieties, as well as gourds. One year, impatient with the wheelbarrowsful with which they were being presented, Don asked Franco what they were supposed to do with them all – unabashed Franco lifted a bottle-shaped gourd from the barrow, sliced off the top and pronounced it to be a perfect candleholder! Don would love to persuade Franco to grow just one variety – the 'Queensland Blue' – which he considers to be the finest pumpkin of all with its dense, sweet flesh. Franco refuses to be persuaded, and so they have to make do with the occasional

'Queensland Blue' among a miscellany of its less-refined and less sought-after relatives, much to their chagrin. There are times when Don and Lindsay wistfully imagine what it would be like to have a gardener prepared to grow what they like eating rather than what he likes growing – but imagining is as far as it gets with Franco in charge. One year Don asked permission to grow a small area of rocket, and also some garlic which Franco refuses to grow. The garlic failed and the rocket quickly went to seed much to Franco's ill-concealed delight. He promptly announced that in future he would grow the rocket as Don clearly didn't have a clue about vegetable gardening. The guests in the apartments, however, are enchanted by Franco and his Vegetable Garden – they wander down and help themselves to salads and vegetables, dreaming as they do so about leaving their busy lives and finding a spot just like this. Maybe, just maybe...

In stark contrast to the other gardens at Venzano, Franco uses a **lot** of water. This is mainly via a Heath Robinson system of pipework that he has rigged up from a trench higher up the slope that is fed by a small spring, but when Don and Lindsay are out for the day he connects up all the hoses and waters to his heart's content. He thinks they don't know. Most of the time it is a fairly harmless activity, but last year he emptied the spring when he forgot to turn the hose off and left it running all night. He must have remembered in the middle of the night because he didn't turn up to work for four days. As this happened in late June, it could have been a disaster, but fortunately the water came back in spite of Franco's misdemeanour.

In addition to being a fine if somewhat unmanageable gardener, Franco is Mazzolla's mushroom expert. Every town in Tuscany has one, whose task it is to offer advice if there is any doubt about the status of a mushroom, but as Tuscany continues to lose quite a lot of people to poisoning, they either fail to consult the experts or not all of them are quite what they purport to be. Franco, however, certainly knows his mushrooms and regularly shares his harvest of fifteen varieties gathered locally with Don and Lindsay.

above (left):
A close-up view of unripe 'Mostro de Firenze' tomatoes still on their vines reveals their beauty.

above (centre):
The swollen pods of borlotti beans will be left to ripen on the plant.

above (right):
A basket of produce from the garden stands ready to be taken to the house.

opposite: *Some chillis are left to dry on the plant to ensure an added fieriness to their flavour.*

The Gravel Garden

O PPOSITE THE VINE WALK, shallow stone steps lead up from the lane to the Gravel Garden, which is laid out in the shelter of the building containing Don and Lindsay's house and the Chapel. A rustic pergola runs the entire length, almost invisible under its extravagantly abundant covering of roses, jasmine and vines which long ago escaped the pergola's supports and headed up across the rooftops. The interior of the pergola is a cool green-lit tunnel where Don nurtures tender shade-loving plants and where visitors can escape the summer sun and climb the steps into the little chapel with its star-studded cerulean ceiling and painted fresco. Sometimes Don or Lindsay find a moment to place a posy of flowers on the altar and light candles – the chapel may be deconsecrated but it is still a perfect place for quiet reflection. Beyond the chapel doors, in a sheltered corner, Don has managed to establish one of his most exotic and transient flowers *Epiphyllum oxypetalum,* the night-flowering cactus, which usually flowers three or four times during the summer. When it is on the point of flowering, evening invitations are issued to friends who come and marvel at the spectacle and luxuriate in its heavenly fragrance - described by Don as "like a giant field of hyacinths". A Volterran resident has become so entranced by the cactus and its mysterious nocturnal flowering that he has twice visited Venzano in the small hours long after everyone had gone to bed to commune with the magical flowers, while a Florentine friend, desolate at never being able to witness the spectacle, was loaned a plant when it was on the point of opening and brought it back three months later!

Parallel to the pergola, the main path of the Gravel Garden runs from the lane to a low wall at the far end, beyond which the land falls away steeply and, framed in the trees, the forbidding fortified walls of Volterra can be seen on the skyline. This is a timeless view, little changed from the days when the monks stood at this same spot and looked out from Venzano as they waited for the bread to bake in the brick-built oven which

opposite: *In the heat of summer the Gravel Garden is a cool green oasis into which you can escape.*

above (left): *A pot of aromatic lavender sits on the step outside the Chapel door.*

above (right): *The Gravel Garden is the main sales area for the Nursery. It is here that customers search out treasures to take home to their own gardens.*

still stands close at hand. Every step taken at Venzano brings one up against the history of this place and little imagination is needed to conjure up visions of those earlier inhabitants.

Lining the path, still further concealing the pergola, aromatic plants and lilies are allowed to grow unchecked and by early summer the air is fragrant with their scent. The exotically beautiful *Hymenocallis littoralis* with its pure white flowers resembling shaggy daffodils emerges from among the shrubs and Venzano's own lavender grows here too – a source of great pride for Don who bred this particular strain and named it after his mother 'June Ellen'. A *pinnata* cross, it has large palmate grey leaves, pale violet flowers and a pleasantly exotic scent. At one point, an ancient *Ziziphus*, or jujube, tree leans across the path – tradition has it that these trees, natives of China, are only found in monastery gardens or gardens of the clergy where they were planted from seed brought back from China by Marco Polo. True or not, it is certainly true that this tree is between 300 and 400 years old, for although *Ziziphus* trees grow quite quickly initially, growth then slows dramatically and it is many, many years before a proper trunk is formed. The small, round fruit taste like apples when green and in September or October turn brown and taste like dates. It is the very last tree to come into leaf and its insignificant green flowers would go unnoticed but for the fact that they smell like an exquisite oriental perfume. There are several varieties of *Ziziphus* each with differently shaped fruit, including one which is like a perfectly-shaped miniature pear. The tree seeds itself readily and not so long ago a local man dropped by and asked Don if he could dig up some of the seedlings. Don happily agreed only to discover him selling them for the equivalent of £10 each in Volterra market. Don now sells them at Venzano himself.

Unlike the other gardens at Venzano that have been established since they arrived, the GravelGarden has been made around a previous garden which had been planted with many trees over the years. The herbs grow

in the shade of a magnificent pine *(Pinus maritima)* which is the favourite haunt of the resident red squirrels who leap about in the tree tops or scurry up and down the trunk as they plunder a nearby almond tree or systematically demolish pine cones in search of the kernels. At the entrance to the garden, two huge false acacias *(Robinia pseudoacacia)* separate the garden from the lane. During late spring when they are in flower, the air is filled with the sound of bees as they constantly visit the white, wisteria-like blossom.

It is in the Gravel Garden more than any other area of Venzano that the abundance of insect life becomes apparent; bees and butterflies are everywhere, iridescent beetles drone ponderously by and angular praying mantis hang around on plants like gawky teenagers at the edge of a dance floor, while during the summer months the incessant buzz of thousands of cicadas is as unrelenting as tinnitus.

The centre of the Gravel Garden is the plant sales area for Venzano, crammed with serried ranks of plants waiting to catch the customer's eye: thyme, rosemary, savory, mint, sage in every shape, size and colour – all jostle for space with lavender, dianthus and other less familiar fragrant plants such as patchouli, vetiver grass and Balm of Gilead *(Cedronella triphylla)*. Balm of Gilead is a tender plant that comes from the Azores and has a warm lemony-balsamic scent which makes wonderful pot-pourri; patchouli and vetiver both originate in India. Although the fragrance of patchouli is now associated with hippies, it was well-known in Europe long before that thanks to its insect-repellent properties. Precious Kashmiri shawls were wrapped with dried patchouli leaves to protect them on the long sea voyage from India to Europe, and for years these shawls would subtly exude the fragrance. In India, the fibrous roots of vetiver are traditionally woven into screens which give off the scent of violets when damp.

For the enthusiast, wandering amongst the herbs is like stumbling upon a treasure trove; for the novice it is overwhelming - which of the 30 lavenders, 25 rosemaries or 35 thymes to choose? How can plants with the same name look so different? With any luck Don or Lindsay will be nearby to reassure the newcomer or make recommendations to the experienced gardener. Everything is grown at Venzano – nothing is bought in – so there are times when particular varieties are not available, but true gardeners, mistrustful of the production-line methods of garden centres, find this reassuring.

In among herbs and tucked under trees and shrubs there are some extraordinary and fairly anatomically detailed terracotta torsoes. The torso-maker is Monica Wapnewski-Plage, a sculptress in her early sixties who resembles an immaculately-dressed 1930's German actress. She normally works in alabaster, but a few years ago decided to do some work in clay and hold an exhibition at Venzano. Don thought there would be half-a-dozen torsoes dotted amongst the foliage with plants tumbling over them, but to his consternation he arrived home one day to find thirty of them dominating the garden! So far they have sold eight and Monica is delighted with the money. She has now returned to working in alabaster and, to Don and Lindsay's great relief, there

be no more torsoes. Don still hasn't recovered from the shock of having the first batch appear in his garden even though they have mellowed with time – Franco has attempted to integrate them into the garden by giving various torsoes interesting hair-styles using ornamental grasses.

Next to their kitchen door Don and Lindsay have a small, shady terrace where they like to sit in the cool of the evening surrounded by some of their favourite and most fragrant plants. Orange and lemon blossom perfume the air, joined in midsummer by the heady fragrance of sambac jasmines. There are four varieties of which Don's favourite is called the 'Grand Duke of Tuscany', it has a completely hemispherical waxy flower and was found in Goa centuries ago by the Grand Duke Cosimo who was also responsible for the collection of hundreds of varieties of lemons which still exist today at the Villa Castello. The intensely double and headily-fragrant flowers start off lime-green, open white and then turn deep pink. On the terrace the Grand Duke is accompanied by his wife 'Maid of Orleans' another sambac jasmine found by him and named after his wife Margarita d'Orleans. The white, tubular, semi-double flowers are equally fragrant and blush pink as they age.

There are other jasmines too – *Jasminum nitidum* which trails delightfully and a lovely South African variety which Don found in Australia called *Jasminum multipartitum* with large, star-shaped rose-pink flowers. Other precious treasures have a home here too – on the table there is a pot of *Zaluzianskya*, a small grey-leaved plant with flowers which remain closed all day showing only the deep pink undersides of the petals but come dusk the flowers open wide to reveal snowy-white indented petals with an astonishingly rich perfume. In spring *Narcissus serotinus,* the smallest of all narcissi yet with a piercing scent has pride of place on the terrace table. At the end of the day with the visitors gone the garden becomes their own and this is where they sit enjoying a glass of wine and discussing the day, weary but content.

above: *The flowers of the night-flowering cactus* (Epiphyllum oxypetallum) *are as exotically beautiful as their perfume.*

right (above): Hymenocallis littoralis *is a bulbuous plant with extremely elegant scented flowers.*

right (below): *A perfect flower of* Jasminum 'Grand Duke of Tuscany'. *In Don's opinion this is the "ultimate" jasmine.*

The Dry Garden

OWN THE LANE past the buildings, the Dry Garden is separated from the others on the south side of the lane by a rough, uncultivated slope (which is destined for development in the next year or so if the eagerly anticipated Australian student proves up to the tasks planned for him). Don and Lindsay established the Dry Garden when they first arrived at Venzano while waiting to start work. It must have been the site of a building at some stage in the past as they found all the stone they needed to build the terraces as they excavated the bank. Although, at the time, it was frustrating not to be working on the house, it gave them the opportunity to really consider how they would develop Venzano, and as Don says, they were quite a lot younger then and had a lot more energy for heavy manual labour!

The Dry Garden has never been watered since it was planted and, although a few plants are lost during very cold winters, it is interesting all year round, albeit somewhat dusty during the summer months. Below the terraced border the gravel path is a self-sown river of vivid purple *Verbena rigida,* opportunistically benefiting from the moisture which collects at the base of the wall. The border itself is planted entirely with Mediterranean shrubs and perennials; there are drifts of cistus and rosemary and a "monk's pepper" (*Vitex agnus castus),* also known as the "chaste tree", an attractive Mediterranean shrub with pretty blue flowers, reputedly so named because monks used its seeds to suppress their worldly "appetites". Beneath the shrubs a beautiful flax (*Linum narbonense)* creates a mist of deepest, richest blue flowers.

Don's favourite plant in the Dry Garden is the gorgeous giant poppy (*Romneya coulteri)* with its white tissue-paper flowers. One evening as he was working in the Dry Garden, a couple of guests wandered down from one of the apartments. They were Deirdre MacSharry, a past editor of the English *Country Living* magazine and her partner Ian Coulter-Smythe and as they admired the garden in the early evening they began talking about the *Romneya.* Ian casually dropped the information that it was his great-great uncle, Dr Thomas Coulter, who had discovered the plant on an expedition through Mexico and southern California between 1829 and 1834. Subsequently, he sent Don a monograph written by Dr Nelson from Trinity College, Dublin, which tells the story of Dr. Coulter's life – as Don says, it is this type of incident that adds richness to their lives at Venzano – if he hadn't happened to be in the garden at that time he would never have heard the story.

The *Romneya's* seeds are notoriously difficult to germinate but following advice from a fellow Australian, Don has persuaded the seeds to do so by the singular method of planting them in a terracotta pot, covering the surface of the soil with pine needles and setting them alight! The usual method of propagating them in Europe is by micro-propagation which tends to produce rather feeble plants. Don learnt this to his cost when he bought a large batch from another grower at the Rome Flower Show for quite a high price with a view to putting them in a client's garden – they all died.

left: *The delicate and fragile beauty of the tissue-paper flowers of* Romneya coulteri, *a giant poppy from southern California.*

opposite (top left): *Don planted this* Pinus pinea *along the lane above the Dry Garden. At the rate it is growing it should not be long before they can harvest their first pine kernels.*

opposite (top right): *It has been quite a struggle to persuade the people of Tuscany to grow cistus in their gardens as they see them growing wild everywhere, but Venzano's improved forms and advice on drought-resistant plants is slowly changing their minds.*

right: Verbena rigida *has seeded itself all along the base of the terrace wall in the Dry Garden where it seems immune to the intense heat of the Tuscan sun.*

Future Plans

FOR THE FUTURE, Don and Lindsay intend to finish what they have planned, as illustrated in Lindsay's lunette on pages 56-7. A series of gardens – all of them different for good reasons – will demonstrate to all who view them the flexibility possible even in this sometimes harsh environment – from the hot Dry Garden to the lush green plants in the Gravel Garden.

At present, their work is concentrated on the Courtyard which has gone through a series of changes since the first day they saw it filled with self-sown trees and undergrowth. Since then it has been a builder's yard, a car park, and overflow plant storage area, but gradually with each alteration it has become less a working area and more a place to linger – soon there will be a pergola at the back of the apartments and along the front of the cow-sheds and its transformation will be complete.

On a wider scale, Don and Lindsay have been determined to help persuade Italian gardeners to adopt native plants for their gardens; for instance, cistus grows wild around Venzano and is little valued, but Don will point out a cultivar and explain that it is a famous variety which comes from Portugal and they become more interested – as long as it is not a variety which grows locally in the woods they can be persuaded to try it and other Mediterranean plants which are, after all, ideally suited to this environment. Educating the public has been a vital part of the process; teaching them to garden with – rather than against – the prevailing conditions, has been essential for customers and clients, all of whom have a problem with water supply. The gardens at Venzano amply demonstrate what can be achieved using many of the often neglected native plants.

right: A singularly vivid planting of Cistus *and* Osteospermum *in the Dry Garden demonstrates that you do not need to choose plants that require endless cossetting with copious watering to achieve a colourful display.*

Converts to their style of gardening visit Venzano's gardens over and over again, each time taking away a few more plants to experiment with, and often expressing surprise at how easy they are to care for. The result is a double bonus; Don and Linday's reputation is beginning to grow and the gardens in the surrounding area of Tuscany are helping to preserve indigenous plants.

PLANT DIRECTORY

A selection of some of Venzano's best-loved plants, with notes on their cultivation, together with
photographs of those that are among the most eye-catching.

Dianthus

CARNATION

Any visitor who arrives at Venzano in early summer when the dianthus are in bloom will be enchanted by these lovely,

incomparably fragrant flowers. While Don and Lindsay have had to adapt the conditions to the extremes of the Tuscan climate,

in most gardens a free-draining, alkaline soil in a sunny spot is ideal.

above: Dianthus anatolicus

above: Dianthus *'Rose di Mai'*

below: Dianthus superbus

'ARABELLA LENNOX-BOYD'

A new variety, created at Venzano, with double pink flowers speckled with a deeper shade of pink. It is a compact plant, 25cm (15in), with a strong perfume.

'BRYMPTON RED'

An antique single variety with flowers the colour of crushed-raspberry and dark crimson eye and petal markings. 30cm (15in).

'DAMASCO'

A long-flowering Venzano introduction. The fragrant maroon flowers are speckled with pink. A compact plant of 15cm (6in).

'JANE AUSTEN'

A compact plant with small single flowers which are red with a white margin. 30cm (15in).

'JANE'S WHITE FRILLY'

Brought to them by their friend Jane who found it in her garden. This antique dianthus has semi-double, fringed white flowers with an intense perfume. 15cm (6in).

'KANDAHAR'

A rather unruly plant with large, toothed, single pink flowers. 50cm (20in), it was brought back from Afghanistan many years ago by a friend of Don and Lindsay.

'QUEEN OF SHEBA'

16th-century single variety. The creamy-pink flowers are feathered and speckled with purple. 15cm (6in).

'ST. AUGUSTINE'

A maroon-flowered dianthus which has been bred at Venzano. It is repeat flowering and reaches a height of 50cm (24in).

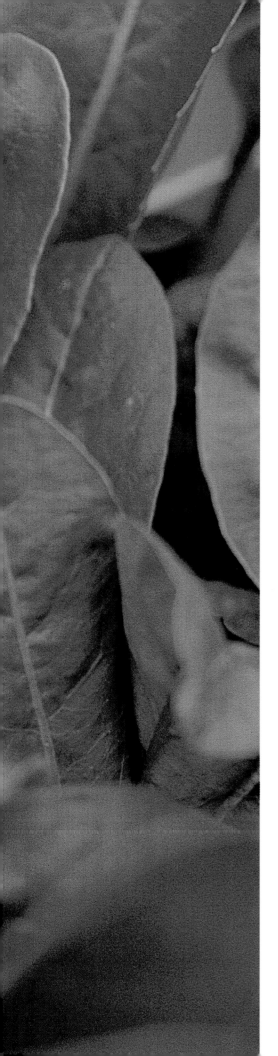

Jaborosa integrifolia

An unusual ground cover plant which originates in Brazil,

it was not thought that it would survive at Venzano but it is now happily

established and has survived temperatures of -15°C (5°F).

Large, tongue-shaped, dark green leaves with night-scented,

star-shaped flowers nestle amongst the foliage. It can be planted in

light shade in well-drained soil, but is also happy in full sun.

above: Jaborosa integrifolia *nestles beneath the stone sink in the Courtyard where it is
clearly thriving in the lightly shaded conditions.*
left: *The pure white flowers that peer from amongst the dense foliage are at their most
sweetly scented at night.*

Jasminum

JASMINE

If Don could only grow one family of plants, he would choose jasmines, especially the sambac varieties which are one of his plant passions. The plants were brought to the West by Arab traders and are sometimes known as Arabian jasmines. The flowers are often used to scent teas. These jasmines are tender and need protection during the winter. Sambac jasmines make good conservatory plants. As yet Don does not sell his favourite 'Grand Duke of Tuscany' which has fully double flowers that start off lime green and then turn white.

NITIDUM
Known as the star jasmine, with white flowers in summer that are delightfully scented. l.5m (5ft).

SAMBAC
Robust climber with dark green leathery leaves and fleshy star-shaped highly perfumed flowers. 3m (10ft).

SIMPLICIFOLIUM VAR SUAVISSIMUM
Straggly twiner with exquisitely scented small white flowers. Summer flowering. 3m (l0ft).

opposite (far left): *Jasminum nitidum*
left (above): *J. simplicifolium* var *suavissimum*
left (below): *Sambac jasmines (*J. sambac*) have leathery green leaves and waxy, intensely fragrant flowers.*

Lavandula

LAVENDER

Of the forty varieties of lavender that are grown at Venzano five emerge as particular favourites. All lavenders need to be planted in very well-drained soil.

DENTATA 'ROYAL CROWN'
A compact dentata with fern-like, toothed, grey-green leaves and rich blue flowers.

'JUNE ELLEN'
A tender lavender bred at Venzano and named after Don's mother. Aromatic, large, deeply-dissected palmate leaves and pale violet flowers. A scent of sandalwood and rose.

NANA ALBA
Described by Don as a "little porcupine" the 15cm (6in) high plant is smothered with round white flowerheads.

PINNATA
Originating from the Canary Islands, this tender lavender will flower all year if kept in a conservatory during the winter. The small flower spikes of intense blue are carried high above the aromatic foliage.

'VENZANO'
A robust *L.lanata* cross, unique to Venzano. It reaches 50cm (20in), and has silver-grey foliage and mauve-blue flowers.

left: Lavandula dentata *has soft, silvery grey foliage and soft blue flowers.*
opposite: *Lavender is irresistible to bees which constantly visit the Gravel Garden from early spring until late in the autumn.*

Lilium

LILY

All the lilies that grow at Venzano are beautiful when they

are in flower but Don has selected four favourites as being of

particular merit for gardeners.

CHALCEDONICUM

The lily that can be seen on Minoan tomb paintings, its scarlet
turk's-cap flowers look at their most effective when planted
with plenty of contrasting green. Stems grow to about 1m (3ft)
and bear as many as 12 flowers.

FORMOSANUM

A white-throated lily from Taiwan, with reddish-purple
or maroon reverse. Grows to a height of 1m (3ft).
Exotically perfumed.

PHILIPPINENSE

A sweetly-perfumed, white-flowered lily from the
Philippines which reaches 80cm (30in). Each stem bears 6-10
flowers which can have red markings on the reverse
of the petals.

REGALE 'ALBUM'

A sweetly perfumed, pure white form of the classic lily.
Easy to grow. l.2m (4ft).

opposite: Lilium regale *'Album' is another flower of simple, perfect beauty,*
but this one is blessed with a delicious exotic perfume.

Lonicera

HONEYSUCKLE

Honeysuckle is a plant which is easy to grow. Its sweet perfume and delicate flowers look particularly lovely

when combined with roses. There is a fine example of the Lonicera etrusca *honeysuckle grown as a*

shrub in the Dry Garden at Venzano.

ETRUSCA

A climber which can reach a height of 4m (12ft). Oval soft-green leaves and fragrant pale yellow flowers during summer and autumn.

IMPLEXA

A native Tuscan plant which Don and Lindsay have seen growing on dry, rocky slopes. Although it can reach a height of 4m (12ft), it can also be grown as a shrub. The perfumed flowers are pink on the inside and red outside and the foliage is evergreen.

Paeonia

PAEONY

The paeonies in the Bulb Garden are all natives of

Europe so they grow very happily at Venzano. The scent

of paeonies is subtle but delicious. They do best in rich,

well-drained soil in full sun or light shade.

MASCULA
Single flowers of pinkish-red followed by attractive boat-shaped seed capsules which split to reveal purplish black seeds. The foliage is dark green with hairy undersides. Height and spread 75cm (30in).

OBOVATA
Single, cup-shaped white flowers with purple filaments. Large deep-green leaves. Height and spread 75cm (30in).

PEREGRINA
Single, bowl-shaped ruby-red flowers. Height and spread 1m (3ft).

above: *The furry seed pods of Paeonia* mascula *before they split open to reveal their seeds.*
opposite: *A perfect paeony flower drenched in early morning dew.*

Phlomis

This distinctive evergreen plant thrives in the hot, dry

conditions at Venzano. The hooded flowers, which are usually

a mustardy yellow, less commonly pink or lilac, are borne in

dense whorls around the stem; the silver grey foliage has a

felty texture and a light coriander scent. Phlomis should be

planted in full sun in free-draining soil – once established

it can tolerate very dry conditions.

CASHMERIANA

A more compact variety reaching 50cm (24in). The grey-green
leaves are lanceolate, with downy grey undersides. The soft lilac
flowers are abundant through late spring and early summer.

GRANDIFLORA

A sizable shrub which can reach 2m (6ft) with broad,
grey- leaves and large yellow flower whorls.

ITALICA

Slightly larger than cashmeriana, this phlomis grows to 80cm
(36in) with lilac-pink flowers. The narrow downy leaves are
grey green and smell of tea when dry.

left: *A large* Phlomis grandiflora *growing in the borders of the
Grey Garden provides colour through late spring and summer although its
mustard-yellow flowers will darken as they age.*

Rosa

ROSE

Through trial and error Don and Lindsay have selected roses which do well in spite of the

Tuscan heat. The majority of these are the climbers which festoon the buildings as well as the surviving

old roses in the Upper Garden and some unusual varieties in the Grey Garden. Roses do best when

planted in a sunny position in heavy soil which is enriched with a slow-release plant food

such as bonemeal, compost or manure.

BANKSIAE VAR. BANKSIAE

Double white form of the delicate Banksian rose it grows to a tremendous height and should only be planted where space is not an issue. Once flowering.

'MME. ALFRED CARRIERE'

A Noisette rose with clusters of well-scented, softly-double white flowers which appear intermittently after the main flowering. It can reach a height of 6m (20ft) or be grown as a large shrub.

'CARDINAL RICHELIEU'

A Noisette rose with clusters of well-scented, softly-double white flowers which appear intermittent

'COOPER'S BURMESE'

Venzano's star performer. The seed for this rose originates from the botanical garden in Rangoon and was first raised at Glasnevin in Scotland. It is tender and should not be grown where temperatures fall below –10°C (14°F). Once flowering, it's pure white single flowers smother every stem for sevenweeks while the glossy, ever-green foliage looks good the rest of the year. Needs plenty of room.

HEMISPHAERICA 'FLORE PLENO'

Cultivated in Europe since the early 17th-century the yellow flowers open into a crinkled yellow globe of petals. It needs a hot, dry climate to look its best, otherwise the densely packed petals tend to droop and rot.

'DE RESCHT'

A highly scented, double crimson rose which is repeat flowering and has proved drought resistant at Venzano.

'SLATER'S CRIMSON CHINA'

The slender pointed buds open to reveal single crimson flowers of great beauty. Rosemary Verey believes this rose is identical to one in a 16th-century painting.

'VARIEGATA DI BOLOGNA'

A charming old rose with a lovely tea-scent. The ivory coloured intensely double flowers are sometimes flushed with soft pink. It reaches 4m (12ft). 4m (12ft) and is repeat flowering.

opposite: *Sweetly fragrant old roses have not been an unqualified success at Venzano, but those that have survived the climate have proved remarkably tough. The rich red petals of 'Cardinal Richelieu' and the candy stripes of 'Variegata di Bologna' make an exquisite picture.*

right: *The little*
prostrate rosemary,
Rosmarinus
'Jackman's Prostrate',
trails attractively over a
low wall, its aromatic
foliage scenting the air
on hot, sunny days.

Rosmarinus

ROSEMARY

This is one of the most important plants at Venzano - there are prostrate rosemaries tumbling over the walls, topiary rosemary in the Dianthus Garden and the Dry Garden has more varieties of rosemary than any other plant. Most prostrate rosemaries are less hardy than the upright varieties and taste too medicinal to be used for cooking. Rosemary grows best in well-drained soil.

'LE COLOMBAIE'
A compact variety reaching a height of no more than 50cm (24in). Suitable for a low hedge. Short, narrow leaves and violet blue-flowers.

'CORSICAN BLUE'
An arching variety of rosemary with deep blue flowers. 80cm (36in).

'GETHSEMANE'
A very small prostrate rosemary which grows no taller than 10cm (4in) with short, dense foliage and bright blue flowers.

'ISRAELI COMMERCIAL'
An erect variety with pale lavender flowers reaching 100cm (45in).

'JACKMAN'S PROSTRATE'
A rare variety of creeping rosemary which grows no taller than 20cm (8in) with green leaves and white flowers.

ROSEUS
An upright rosemary reaching 150cm (60in). Narrow, dense foliage with reddish-green stems and intensely pink flowers.

'VENZANO PROSTRATE'
A creeping rosemary growing to 30cm (16in). Tiny green leaves and intensely blue flowers.

Salvia

SAGE

Like rosemary and phlomis, members of the sage family thrive

in the heat of Tuscany. As well as the usual culinary varieties, they

grow many ornamental sages which have a range of flower colours

from rich blue to terracotta red. Like all Mediterranean plants, salvias

need very free-draining soil, preferably not too rich. Salvias are

tender in colder climates, otherwise they are relatively short-lived

perennials which should be replaced after three or four years. Trim

after flowering to prevent them becoming leggy.

BLANCOANA

From Morocco. Low growing, 30cm (12in), with highly aromatic
small, grey leaves with spires of wedgewood blue flowers in spring
and summer.

LAVANDULIFOLIA

A Spanish sage making a compact shrub of 50cm (20in) with small
narrow leaves and spikes of violet blue flowers in spring. This sage is
ideal for culinary use.

LEUCOPHYLLA

Grey-leafed, highly aromatic salvia from California reaching over 2m
(6ft). Tall spikes of rose coloured flowers in spring and early summer.
Very drought resistant.

RINGENS

A Balkan salvia, to 1m (3ft), with distinctive tri-lobed leaves and long
spikes of dark blue/purple flowers in spring to early summer.

left: Salvia buchananii *has extraordinary 'velvety' pink flowers.* **right:** Salvia sclarea
'Turkestanica' has extremely aromatic leaves as well as particularly showy flowering bracts.

Viola

VIOLET

Among the old strains of violets much loved by Don and

Lindsay for the subtle beauty and ravishing perfume of their

flowers are the Parma violets. Pots of them are tucked on

ledges around their terrace and next to the kitchen door.

Parma violets are tender, best grown in pots in good potting

compost with added leaf-mould. Stand in a shady position

during the summer months and keep well watered. Move into

a frost-free, well-lit place overwinter. Equally attractive is the

little Australian native, V. hederacea.

'CONTE DE BRAZZA'
Double white flowers with a pink shading. Flowers late
winter or early spring.

HEDERACEA
A continuous flowering Australian native, with blotched white
and blue flowers that have a faint scent.

'D'UDINE'
Large, deep violet-blue, intensely scented flowers with white at
the base of the petals. Flowers December to April.

left: *The exquisite Australian native, V. hederacea.*

119

THE NURSERY

& ITS VISITORS

The Nursery Garden

TUCKED BEHIND A ROW of cypresses and bay, adjacent to the Gravel Garden, is the working area where seeds are sown, cuttings taken and potting-up takes place. Inevitably, it is less decorative than the rest of the garden but a good working space is essential in any nursery and it is well-shielded from the visitor's eyes. The curious are discouraged from exploring further by chains hung across the paths from which dangle signs saying *Privato*. During the dreadful winter when for bureaucratic reasons all the plants had to be moved from Venzano Don and Lindsay lost many precious stock plants and it took some years to recover from that blow. Since this low point, things have prospered and now they cannot produce sufficient plants to meet the demand. Even so, in the way of gardening, not everything goes as planned – there have been problems with spring cuttings – especially with the rosemaries and lavenders – possibly caused by the compost they use or the timing. Fortunately, they have discovered that Flavio appears to have a real skill in getting cuttings to root and he now takes them during the autumn.

above: In many ways Venzano is an old-fashioned nursery. Unlike many of its modern counterparts it does not buy in young plants for growing on. The vast majority of plants sold at Venzano are grown from seed that is collected from stock plants, or from cuttings they have taken in the gardens.

opposite (top): Bulbs harvested from the garden ripened ready for replanting.

opposite(bottom): A young Muscari *grown from the bulbs shown above.*

Many plant innovations at Venzano have happened because of accidental placings within the nursery – just putting one plant down next to another can result in a new idea. An example of this was when a batch of pink, blue and white hyssop became mixed together. Deciding that they couldn't be sorted out until they bloomed they were left alone and when they flowered Don realized that the effect was quite wonderful – he often recreates this grouping in the gardens he designs. Then there is the dwarf-leaved myrtle (*Myrtus communis microphylla*) which has proved to be a great success since Don discovered that it naturally forms a globe-shaped bush when grown from seed – these are now grown on into small standards, which have proved to be very popular. As the years have passed at Venzano they have realized it is pointless to try and grow plants which do not do well in this climate – even if they can coax them into life, the chances are that anyone buying such a plant will be disappointed. Instead, they concentrate on plants which relish the Tuscan weather and and which they can confidently recommend to their customers.

The compost, which is used both as a potting mix and a mulch for the borders, is specially made for them by a government-supported programme, whose workers manage the forests to the south of Venzano. Their job is to clean up the forest floor, grind up all the material, compost it and then mix up whatever formula is required. Venzano's compost contains virtually no peat as plants would just dry and die in a peat-based compost in the Tuscan climate; it consists of 70 per cent composted forest material, 10 per cent peat and 20 per cent manure. Getting the balance of the mix is very important for the health of the plants, and Don and Lindsay are hoping that this source will prove a reliable one, since the survival of the young stock is so critical to their success in the nursery.

Once potted, the plants are fed with pelleted manure which has proved very successful although Don has encountered one problem – it always seems to be put on the plants shortly before he has to transport them in the car. Consequently, he often finds himself driving around the Tuscan countryside enveloped in the smells of the farmyard – a fairly unpleasant experience in the heat of summer.

In the past, the geo-thermal power stations to the south of Venzano used to belch out the most marvellous sulphur fumes (Don's words) which were sulphurous, rather than sulphurin, and therefore not harmful to humans or livestock, but wonderful at controlling pests and diseases in plants. He regrets that the EEC has made the power stations put filters in the chimneys to get rid of this smelly but horticulturally beneficial pollution because the roses at Venzano, once disease free, now suffer from blackspot. Their major pest is a tiny flying thrip which infests all the pots of herbs, a problem to which they have yet to find a satisfactory answer, although a wonderful brew has been devised to control aphids – it consists of a one-litre bottle of water, six squirts of liquid hand soap and a small glass of grappa! This is possibly the best use yet for grappa and very, very effective. They have previously experimented with many of the traditional natural controls, such as liquid manures made from nettles, and even cigarette butts, but they all smelled so foul that they gave up on them. The grappa brew, however, remains a firm, inoffensive and successful favourite.

left: Stock plants or new varieties that Don is testing are grown in terracotta pots to avoid confusion with the plants that are for sale which are grown on in more prosaic, but very practical, plastic pots.

New Custom

THE FIRST CUSTOMERS to visit the nursery were English – lured to Venzano by a leaflet that Don and Lindsay sent out to anyone with a non-Italian name in the local phone book. Sadly, as far as they are aware, none of those earliest visitors ever came back, which was hardly surprising as at the time they had hardly any plants to offer for sale.

Still, as word spread among the English residents of the area, customers did start to arrive, curious to take a look at what was going on at Venzano, and gratifyingly eager to buy plants. Soon there was a steady stream of customers of all nationalities – except Italians. With the extraordinary natural beauty of their landscape, the Italians are latecomers to ornamental gardening and, until recently, most have restricted their gardening activities to growing vegetables and the occasional pot of flowers for the balcony or terrace. Don and Lindsay knew that to make a go of the business they had to persuade them to buy their plants, but initially they were at a loss as to how to do this.

Things began to change when Silvia, a freelance journalist from Volterra, asked if she could write about them for the local coastal newspaper which is printed in nearby Livorno. As it happened, the editor of *Gardenia*, the leading Italian gardening magazine, saw the article and decided to ask a contrbuting journalist to do a feature on Venzano. The journalist in question had a favourite great-aunt living in Volterra, so he was delighted to have a reason to spend some time in the area visiting 95-year-old Aunt Nedda and getting paid!

The Fates continued to favour their endeavours as Giorgio Galletti, the director of the famous Boboli Gardens in Florence, read the feature in *Gardenia* and arrived on the doorstep, magazine in hand, before Don and Lindsay had even realized that the article had been published. Since his arrival at the Boboli Gardens, Galletti has masterminded its renaissance. Over many years the gardens, which were first laid out in 1547, had deteriorated into a parlous state but, owing to his great energy and enthusiasm, they are now restored to something closer to their former glory. Thanks to his ongoing visits to Venzano, the island in the lake at the

Gardens is planted with Venzano lilies, the secret garden has many of their aromatic herbs and Don also supplies plants for the 1785 Orangery (which protects rare and tender plants from the frost). The Director is one of their keenest supporters and has been invaluable in introducing them to people of influence within the Italian gardening community.

From those early days when a meagre ten per cent of their business came from Italians and ninety per cent from expatriates, the recommendation of people such as Signor Galletti has brought about a complete reversal of this statistic with ninety per cent of their business now coming from Italians. Landscape gardeners all over Italy now read the Venzano catalogue with enthusiasm and Don has been awarded a Gold Medal for his contribution to Italian horticulture.

The medal in question was awarded to him when he and Lindsay were at the flower show they attend annually just outside Rome. It is held in the extraordinarily beautiful La Landriana garden, which had been lovingly planned and developed by the Marchesa Lavinia Taverna over 50 years. She established the flower show herself and the presentation of the medal, shortly after her death, was an extremely emotional occasion – her husband made a speech which brought tears to the eyes of everyone present – including Don.

The Marchesa was one of the great characters of Italian gardening. She was probably unique in the fact that she spent the first five years in the garden clearing mines left over from the war! Once the 10-hectare (25-acre) garden was safe it was developed with an inspired blend of English and Italian gardening styles, the formality of a classic Italian garden softened by luxuriant English-style flower planting. Much of this was done with the help of her great friend, Russell Page, the renowned garden designer, who added his own inimitable touches to the garden.

The Marchesa was always altering her garden, improving, removing and re-planting. Near the end of her life, she completely changed her much-loved grey border. When first planted, it was backed by young trees and was exceptionally elegant, but as the trees grew larger they began to cast a shadow over it, which affected the hardiness of the plants. For some years she had raised a staggering 5,000 grey-leaved plants each year to replace the losses, but eventually she decided the grey border had to go. Now shade-loving geraniums and hostas thrive in the cool shade, including a stunning planting of *Geranium palmatum* and *G. maderense*, supplied by Don. These geraniums grow up to 1m (3ft) tall and have large, very dissected leaves topped by huge sprays of open-cupped, rich pink flowers during the summer.

Initially, unlike Lavinia Taverna, most Italian customers tended to be very unadventurous when choosing plants, preferring to stick to what they knew. Don and Lindsay's mission was to encourage them to broaden their choice, and in particular to include plants which are native to the region. The "show-and-tell" gardens surrounding Venzano play an important role in this process, especially when Italian gardeners visit them in

opposite: *Don and Lindsay take their plants to a number of prestigious plant fairs that take place in Italy during the spring and autumn. Their stand always attracts a great deal of attention and they seldom find themselves carrying plants back to Venzano.*

left: *The seed-heads of* Zephyranthes candida, *known commonly as "flower of the west wind", provide next year's crop of young plants.*

below: *The pots of* Zephyranthes candida *ready for sale at the Florence Flower Show which takes place each autumn in the grounds of Fattoria le Corti, a l5th-century Medici villa just south of Florence.*

mid-summer. This is the time when the whole of Tuscany turns to dust under the blazing sun, and flowers and foliage wither away unless provided with shade and plentiful water. Yet Venzano's gardens, which have no routine watering, remain green, if somewhat dusty, throughout the summer. Clearly these Australians know what they are doing!

One of the major differences between Venzano and most Italian nurseries is that Don grows his plants from seeds and cuttings. Few Italian nurseries do this, preferring to buy their plants ready-grown from Holland, Germany and France. In the early days when they were first setting up the nursery, Don and Lindsay resorted to importing stock plants because it was so hard to find any in Italy. Ironically, in a reversal of the usual direction of trade, French, Dutch and German gardeners now flock to Venzano to buy plants.

Don attributes his success in this venture to his Australian pioneer spirit with its penchant for breaking new ground. He finds it very amusing that a colonial boy from Sydney's Mosman district is teaching the Italians how to garden!

ZEPHYRANTHES
candida
L. 8.000

Guests and Visitors

ONE OF THE JOYS of Venzano is that the majority of the guests who come to stay in the apartments are people who love gardening – many return time and time again. As lovely as it is, this is no place for family holidays; there is no swimming pool, tennis court, or television and the nearest shops are in Volterra. Those who stay at Venzano are here to escape the hurly-burly. When guests arrive they may intend to visit numerous places in the surrounding countryside, but an enchantment soon falls upon them, resulting in a glorious indolence. They wander through the gardens and occasionally lend a hand, walk through the surrounding countryside marvelling at the wild flowers, sit and read, or even just sit. The idea of joining the masses who queue to visit the sights of San Gimignano, Siena or Florence quickly palls.

Venzano is a place you come to stay when the only sounds you want to hear are the sounds of nature – the wind rustling in the tall grasses, the mellifluous song of the nightingale at midnight and the lazy buzz of insects amongst the aromatic herbs. There is the occasional crunch of footsteps on gravel as someone works in the garden, or an echo of conversation from within the house, while a welcome light breeze may conjure up the gentle, hypnotic sound of wind chimes, but none of these are intrusive. Admittedly there are sporadic seasonal intrusions – tractors ploughing, hunters terrorizing local wildlife and the whine of Franco's strimmer – but these are the sounds of modern rural life, and the silence is all the more profound and enjoyable when they depart, their task completed.

Guests are frequently expert gardeners themselves, often arriving with precious plants as gifts for Don and Lindsay. Bob

above: *Roses wreathe the door to one of the apartments.*

opposite: *Labels in waiting in the nursery.*

Cherry, the renowned Australian plant hunter and nurseryman, has stayed at Venzano and has proved an invaluable help and resource both for Don in Italy and his sister, Kim, in the Hunter Valley. He is a specialist in Sasanqua camellias and has a treasure trove of wonderful specimens in his 22-acre garden north of Sydney, including rare yellow varieties of camellia found on plant expeditions to Vietnam. He recently sent Don a *Lilium nepalense* bulb – a highly prized gift as many of the European bulbs of this striking lily, with its purple-throated lime green flowers, are infected with a virus. One of Lindsay's most recent paintings is of this lily. Thanks to its Australian provenance, it got the seasons confused and flowered in the middle of winter. This turned out to be an unexpected blessing as Lindsay was able to paint it without interrruption. Its unnseasonal display does not appear to have affected it. It went on to set seed fortunately, and its offspring are waited for with great anticipation.

Alongside the guests there is a constant trail of interesting and sometimes colourful visitors. There was an occasion, not long ago, when a grand Italian lady arrived with several Americans in tow. As they toured the gardens she selected numerous plants and, in the course of conversation, she let drop the information that she lived in Chianti and that they made wine on her estate. It was only when Lindsay took Don to one side that he realized that his visitor was none other than Lorenza de Medici. She and her husband have developed their estate in Chianti, Badia di Coltibuoni, where they make legendary wine and where she has established a world-famous cooking school and restaurant. She now frequently visits Venzano to buy herbs.

Friends and Neighbours

IN THE WAY OF REMOTE rural communities there is usually one farmer or smallholder who attracts the hostility of the others. Often it is the newcomers or outsiders, but fortunately Don and Lindsay have escaped this fate although their Sicilian neighbour has not fared so well, incurring neighbours' wrath with his straw-burning activities. Their Sardinian neighbours, however, are hard working farmers who have supported the endeavours of Don and Lindsay since they arrived. Various members of the family often walk down the lane to pass the time of day, particularly Margharita, the grandmother of the family who engages Don and Lindsay in voluble conversation as she berates her husband, complains about official interference or tells of the latest exploits of her identical twin granddaughters who stand wide-eyed next to their *nonna*.

Alessandro Tombelli is one of Don and Lindsay's closest friends and a frequent and a welcome visitor to Venzano. An innovative and talented gardener he collaborates with Don on a number of design projects. As a young man he took himself off to the Royal Horticultural Society College at Wisley to complete a year-long course for foreign horticultural students, undaunted by the fact that he spoke absolutely no English. Don considers him to be one of Italy's finest gardeners: most notably he single-handedly renovated the hedges at the Tuscan gardens of I Tatti and La Foce. Don always commissions him to maintain the hedges and topiary in his clients' gardens and the bay hedges at Venzano also benefit from his sure eye. No sentimental gardener, he takes a fairly tough line with plants and in Don's words, "he can reduce a rose to tears in no time!" During the summer of '98 when Venzano's box hedges were severely scorched by searing heat and drought they were left with a number of unsightly gaps. While Don was prepared to wait patiently for their regeneration, Alessandro's approach was more ruthless. He told Don to "have them all out".

Another of Italy's great gardeners, Joan Tesei, is a tireless ambassador on Venzano's behalf, promoting them at every

opposite (top): *Like most of their neighbours, the local shepherd has warmly welcomed the arrival of Don and Lindsay at Venzano.*

opposite (below): Nonna *Margharita brings her identical twin grand-daughters for one of their frequent visits to Don and Lindsay.*

opportunity. She is one of those people who has popularised gardening in Italy to little personal benefit . It was she who initiated the idea of the La Landriana Garden Show, when she was a consultant to Lavinia Taverna. Don and Lindsay consider her a close personal friend, an unexpectedly wonderful friendship growing out of a shared love of plants. Her own garden near Grossetto on a rocky hill was carved out and planted with characteristic flair and inspiration. She is always trying something new and will often turn up at Venzano laden with treasures, ready to share her bounty with her friends.

Among other good friends around Venzano are Felix and Jane Blunt, who used to be the captain and purser respectively of a large, privately-owned yacht. They would invite Don and Lindsay on board when they were docked at Viareggio – a much enjoyed diversion from the hardships at Venzano. They now own a small farm and an olive mill just the other side of Volterra. Don and Lindsay are delighted to have their friends nearby and equally delighted to get Felix to press their olives. Previously, they had to book an appointment at the local co-op and more often than not, their allocated slot was around three in the morning, when their meagre quantity of olives would be pressed alongside someone else's, meaning potential adulteration. Now it is done at a civilized hour and they know that the oil is all their own.

Venzano has five varieties of olive trees that tend to crop at different rates in different years, so they seldom have the maximum amount they might hope for, but every now and then there is a bumper year. Their record yield so far is 22 litres. When first pressed, their olive oil tastes wonderfully fruity, but is so acidic that it burns the back of the throat. The acidity slowly diminishes so that around four to six weeks after pressing the delicious fruitiness remains but the burning effect has disappeared.

There is considerable rivalry between the various areas of Tuscany as to which one produces the best olive oil. Naturally Don and Lindsay concur with the locals that their region's oil cannot be bettered, the oil from around Lucca being dismissed as

"watery" by comparison. They assess the quality of an oil in the traditional way by sprinkling a couple of drops on the palm of the hand, cupping the hand over the nose to inhale the aroma, and finally licking the palm to taste.

Acutely aware that they owed a debt of gratitude to many local friends and residents, Don and Lindsay decided to throw a party for them in the summer of 1999. It is still the talk of Volterra. In Tuscany, large gatherings are always for family occasions such as weddings and funerals so the event made an enormous impression on their Tuscan friends and neighbours. Don and Lindsay soon realized that they would need to be very strict about who was and was not invited if they were going to keep the party manageable. In spite of several wheedling phone calls and potentially embarrassing confrontations they did not give way and stuck to the original guest list.

It was a beautiful Tuscan evening when the guests assembled in the courtyard, chattering excitedly, admiring the decorations and wandering through the gardens. Don had decided to make a speech to start the evening. On this occasion, he felt his Italian needed some assistance so he enlisted the help of a bilingual friend. When the translation failed to materialize by the evening of the party, he contemplated abandoning the speech altogether. As soon as the would-be translator arrived, he took her on one side, and demanded to know what had happened to his speech. "But I faxed it to you two weeks ago" was her puzzled response. A quick visit to the office revealed the missing speech behind the bookshelf on which the fax machine stands, the guests were duly thanked in their native tongue and went on to enjoy a memorable party. The evening did start on a somewhat disconcerting note when the first arrival was a gate-crasher. Loathe to evict the first guest, they did nothing. Not only was he the first to arrive, he was also the last to leave! He later revealed his identity as a reporter from the local paper by writing a rave review of the party, establishing their reputation as the party-giving supremos of the Volterran social scene!

The Clients

D ON NOW SPENDS far more time than he would like away from Venzano helping clients with the design, landscaping and planting of many prestigious projects. He finds it both a pleasure and a pain. It was not how he and Lindsay had planned their lives in Italy but it brings in substantial earnings, without which they would struggle to keep Venzano going. But the undoubted bonus is that now his reputation is well established, he can pick and choose the projects that he takes on, selecting those that interest him most.

Ornellaia

O NE OF DON'S CLIENTS is a member of a leading Florentine wine dynasty. When he was first given the commission to take on the garden at Ornellaia, it had been landscaped and planted to the design of Arabella Lennox-Boyd, the eminent international garden designer, but was deteriorating rapidly as no-one on the estate was capable of maintaining it. Don arrived to find that the sole custodians were an ex-jockey and someone who had previously worked in the vineyards. He was asked to train them to do the day-to-day work in the garden and once that was successfully accomplished many other projects were passed on to him, including re-designing the entrance courtyard, as well as designing and planting an extensive grey border, the cutting garden close to the house and the new gardens around the cantina - the building where the wine is made.

The Count's house and garden is a place of immense beauty. The house is of seemingly modest

proportions (the extended cellar conceals parking for four cars, and a cinema and the two low buildings either side of the courtyard, although separate, are actually part of the house). Surrounding the house is a series of ravishing gardens, each different but blending harmoniously with the next, which together create one of the most beautiful modern gardens in Italy.

At the front of the house are three extensive terraces – the White Terrace is adjacent to the house, below which is the Blue Terrace, which then leads down to the Rose Terrace. Each has an immaculate lawn of a quality seldom seen in southern Europe, and every border on the three terraces overflows with voluptuous planting in the appointed colours. Beyond these terraces there is an area of lawn planted with specimen trees which in turn leads down to another, even larger, terrace with its classically simple swimming pool overlooking the vineyards and olive groves of Ornellaia with the Mediterranean sparkling in the distance.

One of Don's first tasks was to redesign the area around the *cantina*, where the wine is made. An architectural problem was having a serious effect on the wine-making process. In the centre of the *cantina* is a pentagon-shaped courtyard which was built to conserve a mature oak tree. The walls of the courtyard have large windows and the expanse of glass was allowing the building to overheat. Don was asked to come up with a solution – the result was simple, elegant and highly effective. Mature bamboo plants were planted in front of each of the windows, filtering the light and cooling the building to the correct temperature for wine-making. The Count was delighted, as were the workers in the *cantina*, although Don tired of them asking him when the pandas are going to arrive!

The other gardens around the *cantina* have been equally challenging – in contrast to the traditional-style buildings on the rest of the property, the *cantina* is ultra-modern, so creating the gardens has proved an interesting exercise. Immediately adjacent to the building, Don created two contemporary topiary gardens, while the areas bordering the road and surrounding the car park have been planted with many of his favourite

above: *The re-designed entrance courtyard at Ornellaia includes a fountain and simple blocks of planting.*
opposite: *In the orchard the trees are underplanted with flag iris.*

"dry garden" plants – including rosemary, sage, phlomis, teucrium, California poppies, cistus and lavender. These are planted against a harmonious backdrop of wild cistus, broom and natural woodland, an effect which pleases Don enormously. Not only do these gardens look good, they are extremely low maintenance; they are weeded a couple of times a year and are never watered. Like the surrounding countryside they tend to look dry and lacking in colour in August but the rest of the year they bring colour, shape and texture to an area which would otherwise have little to please the eye.

Don is used to growing plants from seeds or cuttings, so buying fully grown bamboos for the *cantina* was a memorable event. He and the estate manager drove to Vivaio Tor San Lorenzo, Italy's biggest and most famous nursery just outside Rome where all the plants are sold as mature specimens. They entered a forest of 7m (22ft) high pot-grown bamboos and selected 45, which were bought at vast expense and would need to be delivered with a truck and crane. Pleased with the success of this mission, the estate manager suggested they embark on a second. A nearby quarry, he said, would be ideal for the marble needed for Don's suggested fountain in the re-design of the Count's courtyard. Thinking the quarry was on the way home, and still stunned by what they had spent on the bamboo, Don agreed, only to find that the quarry in question was 80 km from Naples. All in all, the round trip took them 18 hours, and Don arrived home exhausted, but satisfied with the results of their extended, and expensive, shopping trip.

above: The Ornellaia gardens consist of a series of colour-themed terraces that surround the house.

Don enjoys an excellent relationship with the Count who, although quite new to gardening, is keenly interested and becomes increasingly discerning as his knowledge grows. He likes to be actively involved in the selection of plants. As they looked at the iris garden together recently, he pointed to some brown-flowered irises and confided, "Don, I'm from the intermediate school of gardening, not the university, and I don't as yet understand the appeal of brown flowers! " These are not the only plants about which he has reservations – the Count has never really come to terms with the olive trees that Arabella Lennox-Boyd incorporated into her design for the garden. Walking round the garden with Don, they came across these particular bugbears. "Look what she had done!" exclaimed the Count, "I'm sick of olives. I grew up with olives. I make olive oil. There are rows of huge, ancient olives everywhere, but she insisted, she said 'Lodovico, this is my design and you will have olives'". Just at this point Don and the Count rounded a corner of the villa to be confronted by a vine growing against a wall. "Grapes! She has put grapes in the ground." Don tried to reassure him, telling him that this was in fact an ornamental vine, rather than just another grape, but the Count remained unpacified.

Although Don is the guiding hand behind the Count's gardens, he is now aided by the head gardener, a bluff Yorkshireman, Nicholas, who has taken to Tuscan gardening like a duck to water. Don was given the task of finding the right person for the job. Little did he think when he left England to grow scented plants that he would find himself training and selecting staff for an Italian count! Finding the right head gardener involved advertising the post, reading endless applications (what gardener wouldn't leap at the

Grossetto

SOME MILES SOUTH OF VENZANO, near Grossetto, Don is engaged on another major project. His clients, Pat and Marcus Meier, a retired investment banker and his wife, are in the process of establishing what they hope will be the world's most comprehensive, organically cultivated, medicinal herb garden. Based on a design drawn up by Pat Meier, it is a garden on a grand scale incorporating over 10,000 plants. Their contact with Don came about via an Austrian nurseryman who had previously bought plants at Venzano, and who thought Don might be able to help them. They duly asked Don to pay them a visit at their new garden and offer some advice. At this stage little more existed than a serpentine path with a few plants dotted around.

It has proved a tough challenge on two counts. Firstly, many of the plants involved are not particularly decorative – in fact quite a few would be considered weeds in other circumstances. However, after some early struggles, Don has found a solution to the problem and has succeeded in integrating these plants into the garden in such a way that the overall effect is enormously pleasing. Although only just over two years old, there are parts of the garden where the planting has achieved an astonishing maturity, and once the surrounding bay hedge has reached its full 2.5 m (8ft) and the young trees achieve more more stature, it will be a truly remarkable garden. At present, the garden does not sit entirely comfortably within the landscape, the meadows and olive groves which surround it and the Tuscan vistas beyond are quite subdued by comparison and are on a larger, less intricate scale. The garden has the appearance of a vivid patchwork quilt that has been flung across the ground – an effect which will be ameliorated once the bay hedge has grown and encloses it.

Secondly, the function of the garden presents a logistical challenge. In order that it works as a physic garden, the plants must be correctly identified and labelled. Having discovered that the labels they had planned on using would cost as much as the plants themselves, the clients opted for a system of numbering the plants, and cross-referring these to a computer plan of the garden, which will then be made into a map for visitors. Although this works in principle, the plants are neither predictable nor is it easy to reach a completion point in the

above: *Don has created a beautiful perfumed garden at the centre of the medicinal herb garden at Grossetto.*

opportunity), selecting those that looked most promising, and flying to England to conduct interviews before making a final selection of two gardeners for the Count to meet. The Count and Don then flew to England together and the final choice was made. As far as Nicholas is concerned he is the luckiest gardener in the world and, visiting Ornellaia, it's hard to disagree. He had spent the past three years learning Italian in Harrogate in the hope that he might one day escape to Tuscany. On the whole, it has been a great success, although Nicholas has had to make a few cultural adjustments. The female staff found his habit of working stripped to the waist disconcerting, and Don was asked to persuade him, tactfully, to cover up. Don's solution was to buy Nicholas a selection of colourful vests which he now wears as he works in the garden, leaving the female staff less troubled.

design of the garden. Don will never be able to say, "That's it – it's finished – you can make your map because nothing will change from now on." Somehow they must devise a system that will allow the plants to be identified, but will also be flexible enough to deal with change within the garden. As often happens, Don has found that he must be as much a diplomat as a gardener, finding a way to accommodate the needs and requirements of his clients with the needs and requirements of the plants.

The medicinal garden covers an area of nearly 3 hectares (7 acres) and is divided into three main areas. Central is the perfumed garden which has a classic Tuscan cypress at its centre, radiating from which are beds of intensely fragrant roses, predominantly *Rosa gallica officinalis* but also 'Quatre Saisons' and the Portland Rose, which in turn are surrounded by four very large corner borders with curved inner edges. These borders are colour-themed and filled with a glorious collection of deliciously scented plants.

On the northern side of the perfumed garden is a physic garden containing a comprehensive range of western medicinal plants as well as a cutting garden incorporating scented plants for pot pourri. Walking round the physic garden is akin to stepping into the pages of an old-fashioned herbal. Here you will find asafoetida, melilot, digitalis, arnica and mandrake among others – herbs that have been used medicinally for hundreds of years are now skilfully planted to be both educational and decorative. Like the gardens at Venzano, bees, butterflies and other beneficial insects abound and the air is filled with the heady scent of aromatic plants.

On the southern side of the perfumed garden is a new garden which is still being laid out. In time, it will contain areas devoted to plants representing a number of different complementary therapies – homeopathy, Ayurvedic medicine, native American herbs, eastern and western plant medicine and aromatherapy. As many of these plants are annuals or biennials, it will not be possible to create the style of permanent planting that predominates elsewhere, but Don is optimistic that with strong and imaginative landscaping this area of the garden will still look very pleasing to the eye.

Casino della Tordella

ONE OF DON'S most exacting clients is Angelina, who employed him to lay out a new area of garden for her at her villa, Casino della Tordella, near Panzano in Chianti. Knowing that she wanted something very special, Don created a design in which rare river stone is used for the main paths, accompanied by matching gravel for the smaller, intersecting paths. The result was really stunning and Don knew it had the makings of a magnificent garden once it was planted. To his considerable consternation Angelina insisted that she wanted the planting done instantly (it was then early summer). Don knew that few of the plants would survive the heat and drought of summer, but he had to comply with her wishes. To his chagrin, the summer was less intense than usual, and that, combined with the mulching effect of the river stones and efficient irrigation, has enabled the plants to thrive, and Don has had, reluctantly, to concede defeat. More worryingly, all her friends now want him to perform a similar miracle on their gardens. Even the river stone and gravel paths have caused him problems, as they have been such a success that his client now wants more of them. Not long ago he arrived at the villa to be confronted by yet another heap of stones purchased at vast expense by Angelina and he now has to work out what to do with them. Success does not always bring its own rewards!

Angelina, too, has had her own problems with the garden. Exceptionally heavy rain combined with an undetected spring beneath the garden undermined the terracing, and the lower half of the garden has fallen away. What was once a beautiful swimming pool surrounded by flower-filled terraces is now an empty hole and muddy slopes. Don arrived at this scene of devastation to find Angelina and a team of helpers rescuing as many plants as possible and planting them in a temporary bed; bloodied but unbowed, Angelina has the engineers and architects planning the rebuilding of the lower garden, and is confident that Don will resurrect her flower borders!

Fattoria le Corti

NOT FAR AWAY from Angelina's villa, just south of Florence, there is the beautiful 15th-century Medici villa of Fattoria Le Corti, the country home of Prince and Princess Corsini. The 500-year-old cypresses in the garden provide the evidence that the garden dates from the same period. The villa is the centre of the family's wine-producing activities and where they grow the olives reputed to make the finest of all Italian olive oils. It is also the venue of the now highly successful Florence Flower Show which takes place over the third weekend in September, and at which Don and Lindsay exhibit and sell Venzano plants.

When they first arrived in Italy the only plant shows that took place were for the wholesale trade, but now there are plenty that are also attended by the general public. At least one takes place each week between the first week of May and the second week of June, after which there is a break for the summer (when it is far too hot for such events) before the shows start again during the first week of September, continuing until the second week in October. Don and Lindsay now attend the best of these, taking the opportunity to meet old friends, new customers and potential clients.

When Don and Lindsay first set out on this odyssey they had visions of a quiet life in a Tuscan backwater where they would spend their days gently pottering amongst plants, but, like all odysseys, the journey has taken a great number of unexpected twists and turns, with the result that Don now finds himself working as a consultant to some of Italy's finest gardens. Twelve years on, with so much greater fluency in the Italian language and an unrivalled knowledge of the Tuscan climate and its effects on the plants, their reputation as gardeners has given them a decided edge in their field of endeavour. To their great delight, the Italians have embraced them, and gardening, with gusto.

Epilogue

THE PICTURE PRESENTED by Don and Lindsay's Italian horticultural odyssey may appear idyllic but it would be wrong to leave readers with the impression that setting up the nursery has been altogether easy. Italian bureaucracy is famously convoluted and long-winded, so it is inevitable that they have had their fill of frustration at the hands of petty officialdom. As they have discovered to their cost, in a country where everyone does their best to remain unnoticed by officials, drawing attention to oneself can have disastrous results. There are so many departments, each with their own rules and regulations, none communicating with one another, that it is impossible to comply with everyone's requirements. Such is the novelty of anyone voluntarily approaching them that the bureaucrats will fall upon the hapless victims and torment them within an inch of their sanity, or further, given the chance.

Don discovered this a few winter's back, when he innocently applied for an export permit for some plants (most would not have bothered). To his horror the officials informed him that not only would they not give him the licence, but that he must immediately remove all commercial plants from Venzano as he did not have the correct paperwork to allow a nursery on the site. There was no point in arguing that he had obtained all sorts of permissions and been given positive encouragement from other quarters; somehow one particular form had been overlooked and officialdom was in hot pursuit. In less Ruritanian conditions, retrospective permission would have been granted, but in this case they would not countenance such a course of action. So it was that, in the middle of winter, Don and Lindsay had to find friends and neighbours who could offer temporary homes for the plants and then they had to deliver their entire stock around western Tuscany. The form duly completed, and permission eventually granted, they took to the road once more and rounded up the surviving plants to bring back to Venzano. It is an episode they would rather forget.

Another eccentric manifestation of Tuscan bureaucracy is the pergola tax. There are few Tuscan villas that do not have a pergola hung with vines, wisteria or roses to provide a shaded alfresco dining area, but in order to avoid paying tax on these structures they have to be "demountable". In other words they must come apart easily and must not be permanent structures. Presumably this came about because of the Italian penchant for building unauthorized extensions to their homes – one day they had constructed a pergola, the next they had added an extra bedroom!

Venzano has a number of pergolas in the gardens and all are demountable. There is also a stack of poles ready for future pergolas which were obtained in a most unusual fashion. One spring afternoon Lindsay was working in the garden when he became aware of a strange noise coming from further up the track. Abandoning his task to investigate further, he found himself watching a man with a large sledge hammer whacking the base of one of the telephone poles. "Who are you, and what are you doing" a puzzled Lindsay enquired. 'Telephone engineer – testing for dry rot. If they make a hollow sound we know they have got it and have to be replaced.' To demonstrate, he whacked the base of the pole again, and it promptly toppled sideways, leaning at a crazy angle, supported by the wire alone. Unconcerned, the engineer moved on to test the next pole, leaving Lindsay to hurry back to the house to check whether they still had a functioning line. Once they had come to terms with the eccentricity of the method, Don and Lindsay realized that although the condemned poles may have outlived their current usefulness, they would, nonetheless, make perfect pergola poles. A casual enquiry to the engineer about their disposal led to Don and Lindsay generously offering to get rid of them – leaving everyone happy with the outcome.

Suppliers

VENZANO CLIENTS

Garden designers

Marchesa Giuppi Pietromarchi *(Tuscany)*
Paolo Pejrone *(Turin)*
Arabella Lennox Boyd *(international)*
Joan Tesei *(Tuscany)*
Anthea Gibson *(U.K.)*
Oliva di Collobiano *(Florence)*

Public Gardens, Hotels etc.

La Landriana *(Rome)*
Boboli, Castello & Petraia Gardens
(Florence)
Orto Botanico *(Florence)*
Orto Botanico *(Rome)*
Hotel Villa San Michele *(Florence)*
Hotel Splendido *(Portofino)*
Commune di Siena
Villa i Tatti *(Florence)*

Private Gardens

Donna Marella Agnelli *(Corsica / Turin)*
Marchesa Bona dei Frescobaldi *(Florence)*
Tenuta dell'Ornellaia *(Tuscany)*
Marchese Giuseppe di San Giuliano
(Sicily)
Contessa Sanminiatelli *(San Liberato)*
Lord & Lady Cavendish *(Tuscany)*
Arnaldo Pomodoro *(Milan)*
Federico Forquet *(Cetona)*
Hugh Honour *(Lucca)*
Tom Parr & Klaus Scheinert *(France)*
Lord Lambton & Clare Ward *(Tuscany)*
Adam Pollock *(Tuscany)*

Additional notes

Feature about Don in the Australian
Magazine 11-12th September 1999 by
Lisa Clifford Consumi.

BIBLIOGRAPHY

Guide Books to the Area:

Blue Guide to Tuscany by Alta Macadam
*(A & C Black London, WW Norton New
York)*

Cadogan guide to Tuscany, Umbria & the
Marches by Dana Facaros & Michael
Pauls *(Cadogan Guides, London distr. North
America by The Globe Pequot Press)*

Books on Scented Plants and Herbs:

Scented Plants by Roger Phillips &
Martyn Rix *(Pan Publishing)*

Scent in your Garden by Stephen Lacey
(Frances Lincoln)

Royal Horticultural Society Encyclopedia
of Herbs and their Uses by Deni Bown.

The Fragrant Herb Garden by Lesley
Bremness & Clay Perry *(Quadrille)*

Herbs by Roger Phillips & Nicky Foy
(Pan Publishing)

The Scented Garden, Rosemary Verey
(Frances Lincoln)

SUPPLIERS

UNITED KINGDOM

*Following is a list of specialist nurseries and
garden centres catergorized according to plant
speciality. This list is not exhaustive and it may
be worthwhile to consult your telephone
directory or a website listed below for a plant
centre in your area.*

Dianthus

Southview Nurseries
Chequers Lane
Eversley Cross
Hook, Hampshire RG27 0NT
Tel: (0118) 9732206
(mail order only)

Herbs

Alexandra Palace Garden Centre
Alexandra Palace Way
London N22 4BB
Tel: (020) 84442555
Email: sales@capitalgardens.co.uk
Website: www.capitalgardens.co.uk
Bodmin Plant and Herb Nursery
Laveddon Mill
Laninval Hill
Bodmin
Cornwall PL30 5JU
Tel: (01208) 72837
Brin Herb Nursery

Brin School Field
Flichity, Inverness
Highland IV2 6XD
Tel: (01808) 521288
Cheshire Herbs
Fourfield
Forest Road
Nr. Tarporley
Cheshire CW6 9ES
Tel: (01829) 760578
Web addess: cheshireherbs.com
(mail order seeds only)
Hollington Herb Garden
The Walled Garden
Woolton Hill
Newbury
Berkshire
Tel: (01635) 253908
Iden Croft Herbs
Frittenden Road
Staplehurst
Kent TN12 0DH
Tel: (01580) 89143
Email: idencroft.herbs@dial.pipex.com
Website: www.herbs-uk.com
Jekka's Herb Farm
Rose Cottage
Shellards Lane
Alveston
Bristol BS35 3SY
Tel: (01454) 418878
(Mail order only)
Poyntzfield Herb Nursery
Nr. Balblair
Black Isle
Dingwall
Ross and Cromarty
Highland IV7 8LX
Tel: (01381) 610352
The Herb Farm
Peppard Road
Sonning Common
Reading
Berkshire RG4 9NJ
Tel: (0118) 9724220
Website: www.herbfarm.co.uk
The Cottage Herbery
Mill House
Boraston
Nr. Tenbury Wells
Worcestershire WR15 8LZ
Tel: (01584) 781575
Trent Cottage Herbs
Trent Nurseries

56 Tittensor Road
Tittensor
Stoke-on-Trent
Staffordshire ST12 9HG
Tel: (01782) 372395

Lavender

Downderry Nursery
Pillar Box Lane
Hadlow, Tonbridge
Kent TN11 9SW
Tel: (01732) 810081
Email: simon@downderrynursery.co.uk
Website: www.downderrynursery.co.uk
Norfolk Lavender
Caley Mill
Heacham,
King's Lynn
Norfolk PE31 7JE
Tel: (01485) 570384
Email: admin@norfolk-lavender.co.uk
Website: www.norfolk-lavender.co.uk

Lilies

Broadleigh Gardens
Bishops Hull
Taunton
Somerset TA4 1AE
Tel: (01823) 286231
Website: www.broadleighbulbs.co.uk
(mail order only)

Roses

Curbishley's Roses
Bate Heath
Aston-by-Budworth
Northwich
Cheshire CW9 6LT
Tel: (01565) 733286
(no mail order service)
David Austin Roses
Bowling Green Lane
Albrighton
Wolverhampton WV7 3HB
Tel: (01902) 376377
Website: www.davidaustinroses.com
Flyer's Roses
Manchester Road
Knutsford
Cheshire WA16 0SX
Tel: (01565) 755455
Email: rosesales@fryers-roses.co.uk
Website: www.fryers-roses.co.uk

Harkness Roses
Hitchin
Herts SG4 0JT
Tel: (01462) 420402
Email: harkness@roses.co.uk
Website: www.roses.co.uk
(mail order only)

Unusual and aromatic plants

Avon Bulbs
Burnt House Farm
mid-Lambrook
South Petherton
Somerset TA13 5HE
Tel: (01460) 242177
Website: www.avon-bulbs.com
(mail order only)

Crug Farm Plants
Griffith's Crossing
Caernafon
Gwynedd LL55 1TU
Tel: (01248) 670232
Website: www.crug-farm.co.uk

Cotswold Garden Flowers
Sands Lane, Badsey, Eversham
Worcestershire WR11 5RZ
Tel: (01386) 422829
Email: cgf@star.co.uk
Website: www.cgf.net

Spinners Nursery
School Lane Boldre, Lymington
Hampshire SO41 5QE
Tel: (01590) 673347
(no mail order service)

Useful websites
www.e-garden.co.uk
for buying online and gardening advice
www.oxalis.co.uk
comprehensive UK listing of gardening resources
www.herbsociety.co.uk
online herb resource and organisation

AUSTRALIA

Cottage Herbs
Lyndon Rd
MacDonald Park SA 5121
Tel: (08) 82847988

Country Thyme Herbs
Lot 40 Farrall Rd,
Midvale WA 6056
Tel: (08) 92748608

Fancy Foods Hunter Valley Herb Farm
Depot Rd, Merriwa NSW 2329
freecall 1800 069 516
Tel: (02) 65482314

Herbscape
4 Boscastle Ave
City Beach
WA 6015
Tel: (08) 93858498

House of Herbs and Roses
745 Old Northern Rd
Dural NSW 2158
Tel: (02) 96511027

JA's Herb Nursery
81 Flaxton Rd
Mapleton QLD 4560
Tel: (07) 54457128
Fax: (07) 54786185

Just Herbs
8 Manning Rd
Aberfoyle Park SA 5159
Tel: (08) 83705876

Lan Daem Herbs
PO Box 98
Latrobe TAS 7307
Tel: (03) 64284182

Perennial Charm Nursery
Hoopers Road
Barmah
VIC 3639
Tel: (03) 58693227

Plant Treasures of Polkobin
Lot l3, Gillards Road
Polkobin
NSW 2320
Tel: (02)49987207

Shipards Herb Farm
Windsor Rd
Nambour QLD 4560
Tel: (07) 54411101

Tahara Bridge Homestead Herb Farm
RSD 7200
Coleraine VIC 3315
Tel: (03) 55754257

Woodbank Nursery
2040 Huon Road
Longley
TAS 7150
Tel: (03) 62396452

Useful websites
www.herbsaustralia.com.au
comprehensive Australian directory for herb growers, suppliers and nurseries
www.pleasanceherbs.com.au
online advice and mail order specializing in herbs

NEW ZEALAND

Bay Bloom Garden Centre
PO Box 502
Tauranga
Tel (07) 5789902
Fax (07) 5779752
Website: www.baybloom.co.nz

Gardenways Garden Centres
Branches throughout Christchurch
Tel: (03) 3853899 for nearest location

Herbs Lavender Heaven
89 Waitara Road
Brixton
Waitara
Tel: (06) 7548848

Kings Plant Barn
Takapuna, Tel: (09) 4432221
Milford, Tel: (09) 4109726
Remuera, Tel: (09) 5249400
St Lukes, Tel: (09) 8462141
Howick, Tel: (09) 2738527
Website: www.kings.co.nz

McCully's Garden Centres
Branches throughout Christchurch
Tel: (03) 3517128 for nearest location

Oderings Nurseries
Branches throughout Christchurch
Tel: (03) 385238 for nearest location

Palmers Gardenworld
Head Office:
182 Wairau Road
Glenfield
Auckland
Tel: (09) 4439910
Branches throughout the North Island

Simply Herbs
159 Tirau Street
Putaruru
Tel: (07) 8833727

Wairere Nursery
Gordonton Road RD1
Hamilton
Tel (07) 8243430 or freephone: 0800 767354

Useful websites
www.gardens.co.nz
comprehensive advice and online mail order service
www.plantfinder.co.nz
Online mail order featuring 39,000 plants and seeds

SOUTH AFRICA

Botanical Society of South Africa
Kirstenbosch, Cape Town 7735
Tel: (021) 7972090

Blackwoods Herbs
PO Box 6078
Uniedal 7612
Tel/Fax: (021) 8891002
Email: mvweaver@iafrica.co.za

Dunrobin Garden Pavillion
Old Main Road, Botha's Hill
Tel: (031) 7771855
Fax: (031) 7771893

Grey Heron Nurseries
Langeberg Road, Langeberg Ridge
Durbanville
Tel: (021) 9887670 / 9124

Keith Kirsten's Bedfordview Nursery
92 Concorde Road East
Bedfordview 2007
Tel: (011) 4554000
Fax: (011) 4556361
Website: www.keithkirsten.co.za

Lifestyle Family Garden Centre
Corner of DF Malan and Ysterhout
Avenue
PO Box 2568
Northcliff 2115
Tel: (011) 7925616
Fax: (011) 7925626

Margaret Roberts Herbal Centre
PO Box 41
De Wildt 0251
Tel/Fax: (012) 5041729

The Garden Centre
Kirstenbosch Botanical Gardens,
PO Box 195, Newlands 7725
Tel: (021) 7621621
Fax: (021) 7620923

Useful websites
www.nbi.ac.za
comprehensive website from the National Botanical Institute of South Africa
www.garden.co.za
general gardening information and online mail order

Index

Acknowledgements

PHOTOGRAPHY CREDITS

The transparencies in this book were specially taken by the following photographers who individually own the copyrights to their work:

t/b (top/bottom) • l/r (left/right) • tl/tr (top left/top right) • bl/br/bc (bottom left/bottom right/bottom centre) • c (centre)

Stephanie Donaldson copyright c: front cover b, pp 20, 21, 40-41b, 46-47, 50-51, 52-53, 81, 89t, 91b, 114-115, 125, 129

Michelle Garrett copyright c: back cover and flaps, pp 2t, 6bl, 6br, 8, 9, 10, 14-15, 16b, 22c, 22r, 23, 25b, 28, 31, 35r, 36-37, 39tl, 39bl 39br, 41tl, 45, 49l, 59, 60, 61, 62, 63, 64, 65, 66, 69, 72-73, 76-77, 79r, 85l, 86, 87, 92-93, 96, 97t, 98, 99, 107, 108-109, 118-119, 124, 131b, 132, 133, 134, 135, 139

Sue Snell copyright c: front cover t, spine, pp 2b, 6-7, 6bc, 7l-r, 11, 12-13, 16t, 18-19, 22tl, 24, 25t, 26, 27, 29, 30, 32-33, 34, 35l, 38, 39tr, 40tl, 42, 43, 46tl, 48, 49tr, 53tr, 54-55, 58, 67, 68, 70-71, 73r, 74, 75, 78, 79l, 80l, 82, 83, 84, 85r, 88, 89b, 90, 91tl, 91tr, 94-95, 97b, 100, 101t, 101b, 102, 103, 104-105, 106, 109r, 110-111, 112, 116, 117, 120-121, 122, 123, 126, 127, 128, 131t, 137, 140

THANKS

Above all, my thanks go to **Don and Lindsay** who have tolerated my intrusion into their lives with a grace and charm that has allowed an enduring friendship to develop. Many thanks are also due to **Sue Snell** and **Michelle Garrett**, whose photographs so successfully interpret the beauty of Venzano and its surroundings, to **Susan Berry** for editing the book with a light, but deft touch and to **Debbie Mole** for her inspired design skills. And finally my thanks to **Yvonne McFarlane and her team** at **New Holland** for making it possible to write this book.

ABOUT VENZANO

For those who would like to visit Venzano, you should get in contact with **Don Leevers and Lindsay Megarrity at Venzano, Loc. Mazzolla, 56048, Volterra (P1), Italy.** The email address is **venzano@sirt.pisa.it** The **nursery is open** each year from **1 March to 15 December** and the **opening hours** are from **Thursday to Sunday (10-6pm, closed from 1-2pm).** A **catalogue** of plants is available for **5000 lire plus postage,** but there is **no mail order.** The major plant fair near Venzano is at Giardini in Fiera, San Casciano, Florence during the third weekend in September. **APARTMENTS** There are **three apartments** to rent from **1 April to 1 November.** There are two one bedroom apartments and one two bedroom apartment. Each has a living room, private terrace, separate bathroom and kitchen. **DIRECTION** To get to Venzano by air, the **nearest airports are at Pisa** (the most convenient) and **Florence,** but you can also **drive from Rome (4 hrs),** Bologna (3 hrs) or **Milan (4-5 hours).** To find Venzano by road, it is 10km from Volterra in the direction of Colle val d'Elsa, turning off this road to Mazzolla.